Dancing Under Evergreens

A Vietnam Veteran's Wife's Experiences and the
Trials and Hope that Followed

Frances C. Hansen

BookLocker
Trenton, Georgia

Print ISBN: 978-1-64719-926-5
Ebook ISBN: 978-1-64719-927-2

Published by BookLocker.com, Inc., Trenton, Georgia.

Printed on acid-free paper.

BookLocker.com, Inc.
2022

First Edition

Library of Congress Cataloguing in Publication Data
Hansen, Frances C.
Dancing Under Evergreens: A Vietnam Veteran's Wife's Experiences and the Trials and Hope that Followed by Frances C. Hansen
Library of Congress Control Number: 2021923075

Acknowledgments

This is a memoir. I thank my children, Tanya, Christopher, and Michael, who lived through it all with us. They were there to help endure the trials.
Thanks goes also to God who was faithful all the way.
He never changes.
I would be remiss not to mention David, Thomas, and Rabbecah, my other three children of Philip's. Their thoughts and support through everything were so appreciated.

Contents

Chapter 1:
From Rice Paddies to Hospital Wards

Leeches clung to him as he sloshed through the marshy waters. The heat was sweltering in what was known to be sunshine country. Days seemed endless. The time finally came to cross off the last day on his short-timer's calendar. Some were not as fortunate, but he made it through the last twenty-four hours. He went home to uncertainty. He never understood the paradox of walking down the streets of Oakland, California in his cammies, eating an ice cream cone only hours after he was in the jungle. The young medic never stopped wondering why the bullets that whizzed by his head on countless occasions never hit him. He wondered why he had made it out and others had not. Survivor guilt was at its finest. He left home as a conscientious objector and returned as a tried-and-true combat veteran.

Life began in October of 1948 at Kings County Hospital in Brooklyn, NY He was the son of Danish immigrants. His mom was forty when he was born. He remembered being referred to as a "change of life" baby. He also remembered his mom's story about how she came to this country. In her thick Danish accent, she told him several times. "One night, there was an angel in my room." She spoke of her home in Aalborg, Denmark.

"There was a voice that spoke to me."

"You will come to a strange country."

Not long after that, she met Emil Hansen, from Copenhagen. He had already ventured once to the United States as an eighteen-year-old. He worked his way across the country doing odd jobs. Upon his return to Denmark, he found his wife, Marie, and they made their way together back to the states.

Philip was one of five, and the only boy. Growing up in Brooklyn, he lived in many neighborhoods. His dad was an apartment building superintendent. Early days consisted of walks with his dad to Coney Island, and rides on the ferry to Staten Island.

He was also busy with good deeds that his dad taught him to do for those in need. Sometimes they would take his youngest sister. They shoveled the driveway for a bed-bound friend, took groceries to people, and whatever other needs Emil found. They were loyal Lutherans who attended the Salem church in Brooklyn. It was predominantly attended by Scandinavians at the time. Services were sometimes held in Danish and English.

He talked of the frugality of his dad. One example was when he was in the bathroom and dad heard the toilet paper roll unravelling.

"Philip-manna!" He was often rebuked for using too much toilet paper. He explained that he was called by that name all the time. It was an affectionate term his parents daubed their little man.

In his teen years, Phil teamed up with a couple of his buddies. He worked at a pharmacy in Manhattan and sold magazines. The three amigos would frequently hop the subway and go all over the city. Before he was old enough to go into the service, the family moved Upstate to the little hamlet of New Lisbon, not far from baseball lover's Cooperstown. The lived in a red and white colonial near plants, streams for fishing and woods for hunting. His parents raised chickens and had a few goats that liked to run away. Phil didn't dare go on the property of the neighbor. That man threatened kids with the thought of getting shot if they trespassed.

In 1967, at the age of nineteen, he was in the Army. His buddies went too, but in other branches. Over the years he lost touch with them. He wasn't sure where they landed, but he went to Vietnam. After being a cook in Texas for Uncle Sam, it was his turn to go overseas. He obtained his conscientious objector status. An agreement had to be written with much forethought, signed by the pastor, and agreed to by all parties. The young blonde, like many of his cohorts, was part of the main thread of America. His world of ethics was made of God, apple pie, hot dogs, and family. He certainly was not going to take up arms. He was going to Vietnam as a medic. His pastor pronounced a special bible verse over him at his confirmation at the age of fifteen.

"Be ye steadfast, immoveable, always abounding in the work of the Lord." In his belief system, this did not include taking up arms.

After entering the country of Vietnam, which he referred to as Shangri-La, it quickly became apparent that it was unsafe not to carry a weapon. It was "Kill or be killed." He changed his mind and took up arms. He told many stories about hearing screams as others were wounded.

"Medic!" He related how he ran out to help, with his medical kit and supply of morphine ampules. Hot bullets flew past his head. He was with the First Cavalry, Eighth Engineers. The TET offensive was coming to an end. Medic duties intertwined with engineering tasks. He and others were dropped down into thickly wooded areas of the jungle. After the chopper dropped them in, the engineers had to strap C-4 explosives to the trees to blow them up. Landing zones had to be made for the choppers. Aside from explosives blowing up trees, planes flew overhead dropping defoliants to rid the trees of the leaves that created the jungle thickness. One such famous chemical was called "Agent Orange." He spoke of it falling on his skin and on his food.

Sixties songs played on the radio, as seen in some movie clips. He was aloof telling his stories of officers who got "fragged" because the guys didn't like them. Fragging was the deliberate killing of a military officer. I cringed at some of these stories. There are still others that he and his vet friends told me that I have never repeated. There was a lot of condemnation put on the Vietnam vets. I thought of it in a different way. I considered that if I, or anyone else was put into that situation, we couldn't predict ahead of time how we might cope, or what we might do. With that frame of mind, I was able to become a good listener when he finally decided to open up about it.

I still have the rusted pieces of shrapnel that he brought home in an envelope. He also had an old first aid kit, complete with gauze and a morphine ampule. I don't know what he eventually did with it. It disappeared years later, along with the plain silver bracelet he wore all the time. He told me the Montagnards gave it to him. They were a tribal people that he sometimes worked with.

When I first met him, Vietnam seemed a trivial matter in his life. He had been there. He had been a medic. That was the end of the story. When he got home, which was nine years before I met him, he moved north to Rochester to live with his sister and family. It became a family joke about all the jobs he had in a short time. He would get fed up and quit. He always said he was a man of principle. He wasn't going to put up with any farce. Back in Brooklyn, he quit high school three times. He once wrote about some of his antics there. Once he and his friends dumped a colorful supply of paint out of the school window. Primary colors mixed on their way down the bricks on the side of the school. He eventually earned his GED. He always bragged about attending the same high school as two famous singers.

In Rochester, he recalled his first date since returning home. They went to play tennis. He didn't understand why, but he was angry playing that game.

"I was so angry. Every time it was my turn to hit the ball, I slammed it back as hard as I could. I didn't know why I was so angry. That was the last time I ever dated her."

In his Army days, with the persuasion of some of his buddies, he decided to become a Mormon. He continued to ignore his Lutheran upbringing and joined the Mormon church. It was there that he became a Seventy, which is a high position in that denomination. He married his first wife in a temple, where he was given a secret name. He wore the special underwear that they were told to wear, consisting of a silky fabric top and boxer-style shorts made of the same fabric. He said he was told that if he ever divulged his secret name to anyone, he could be struck dead. He told me his name was Alma and his wife's name was Dorothy. He also had the odd privilege of baptizing the dead, a ceremonial ritual reserved only for those with special callings. He told of his missionary days as an early Mormon where they were taught to say certain things to sell the religion to those they visited.

He met and married that first wife at the young age of twenty-one She was a good Mormon girl. In remaining true to their beliefs of having many children to bring the spirit babies into the world, they soon had three children. Things started to get tough. Money was tight and she insisted that he work more. He took on two jobs.

Shortly into their separation, before I knew him, Phil decided he wasn't going to lose custody of his children. His wife already had him sleeping in the attic before he moved into the room he rented. He decided he was going to take his boys. He believed that the youngest, a girl, should be with her mother. The children were approximately ages five, three and two. He traveled to Lancaster, Pennsylvania, rented an apartment, furnished it, and came home to take his boys there. He said that on his way, he wrote some bad checks. His inbred Lutheran conscience caught up to him. He decided to turn around, returning all the money to the banks and brought the children home.

It was truly amazing that he didn't land in jail over the incident. Understandably, his former wife never trusted him again. She was always making sure her new husband escorted Phil and the kids to the park on his visitation days. One time, after we were together, she and her husband interrogated Phil on their front porch with plenty of questions, taping every word. The vendetta continued. He always had to fight to see his kids. His heart was ripped apart over the situation.

When I met him, he was separated, living in a room he rented in a large house in the city. He worked as a respiratory technician at the University of Rochester hospital. He also worked as an industrial spy for a gasoline survey company. This involved driving around to the gas stations in the city during the night and writing down the prices of the gasoline at each place, then submitting it to the parent company. When he first told me about this, I thought he was somehow connected to the underworld. I never heard of such a thing. It sounded sneaky to me. One night, after we started dating, he took me on one of his spins. Driving around the city, he checked numbers on the gas pump and wrote them down. To this day, when I hear the name of that survey company on the radio, I just smile.

We worked on the eighth floor of Strong Memorial Hospital where the medical and surgical intensive care units were located. I was a new nurse working on the surgical end. I met him on the night shift. Margo, the other nurse, introduced us.

"Phil, this is Fran. She's new to Rochester."

I politely responded. I had already noticed him. His Scandinavian tan and tousled dirty blonde hair caught my attention when he strolled confidently into the unit. He was wearing white scrubs and carrying someone's oxygen tubing. It was the Brooklyn accent that grabbed me. I had several friends from New York in college and I had fallen in love with their accent. He soon learned that I didn't know my way around the city. He pulled his black book out of his pocket and spoke with that smooth New York voice.

"I'd take you around, but I'm booked up for a couple of weeks." He said as he looked at his calendar.

"How about it if I take you around in two weeks? I'll take you out to lunch or something." I sheepishly consented, excited about the prospect, but somewhat leery about this tan sultan. Margo told me he was dating a couple of the nurses from the medical ICU at the other end of the hall.

"We're going to Hamlin Beach. Then we're going over to her house and I'm going to make Jambalaya."

I was never one to stay quiet for long. The words just came out of my mouth to this stranger.

"Who are you, the social activities chairman for Strong Memorial Hospital?"

We all laughed, and he returned to his little office on the eighth floor, between the two units.

Two weeks went by. I decided to visit my brother in Saratoga Springs. The Boston Pops were scheduled to be at the Saratoga Performing Arts Center. It was late June. I was excited. I was finally on my own. I had my apartment, my Chevy Malibu, and a good paying job that gave me four weeks of vacation the first year. Driving down the New York thruway I thought I owned the world. The concert was great. It was outside. While my brother was escorting an actress to her seat, I was enjoying the music. After the great weekend, I drove back to Rochester, just as exuberant about life as I had been when I left. My shifts at the hospital were rotating days and nights. I knew I had some time to relax before I had to go in.

Dragging my overnight case down the steps to my basement apartment, I noticed something sticking out of the number plate on the door. It was a yellow envelope with my name and apartment number written on it. In the upper left-hand corner were the letters, "P. J."

"Enjoy the weekend," was written on the back flap. It was sealed. I couldn't open it soon enough. I knew who it was from. I hadn't seen him lately and the date was still a week away, but he had been on my mind constantly. Curiosity took over. There was a poem inside. It was hand-written, on yellow lined paper.

"Fran...
Whatever it was
"It can't be denied.
Though some think it rash
And others use it to lie.
I know yours was true
...Two shadowed eyes confirmed.
So what are these words spent on you?
Just about a smile I hope to earn.

Fran seems to lark with a smile
that I find becoming... inviting.
Then after six days you and I
to share the sun and air and the birds will sing."

I was baffled and delighted at the same time. My thoughts raced. I thought it was strange that this guy with a little black book who said he was so busy over the next couple of weeks hadn't wasted any time getting this note to me so soon after we met. I went about my business, and we saw each other in passing at work. Our shifts didn't always match. We both worked the day and night shift rotation.

Soon the date day was upon us. I didn't like his outfit when he picked me up. Frankly, I would rather have looked at him in his white scrubs. He wore polyester pants with a short sleeved knit shirt that didn't match. I pushed it to the back of my mind when I saw the muscular arms beneath the sleeves. I had never played miniature golf. He taught me how to hit the ball under tiny churches and scaled waterfalls. I lost, but I learned the game, and we had fun. Then he took me to lunch at a Mexican restaurant. We had a lot of talking and laughing to do. I spilled my glass of water. Despite my complete embarrassment, I remained calm while the waitress cleaned it up. Later, he told me that he had been impressed by my poise when I spilled the water. Instead of getting flustered, I had remained calm, and that impressed him.

He took me to a local park for a while and that was the end of our date. He had to get to his second date of the day. I was flabbergasted. Two dates in one day! This guy really was a Casanova. Not long after that he called and set up our second date. He knew how much I loved to dance. He set us up for dinner and dancing at a local

Ramada Inn near the airport. There was going to be a live band.

Strangely, I was already hooked. I planned wisely for the date, purchasing a stylish red suit made of soft jersey fabric that swayed, and a pair of black strapped wooden heels that were made in Italy. It was the style of the disco days. When he picked me up that night he was finally dressed nicely. Dinner was great and we danced until the band finished playing. I guess it wasn't love at first sight, but that night something changed.

It was like heaven and earth moved. I can still remember the look in his eyes as we danced to the smooth jazz music.

It wasn't long before he was coming over to my apartment all the time with his typewriter. We discovered that we both loved to write. I had nothing published at that point, but we would critique each other's writing. Once he had several pages written about a story that involved a large group of people getting stuck in an elevator. I thought it was a great story, until he decided it wasn't and tore it up. He was always writing me poems, at home and at work, on X-ray cardboard or doctor's progress notes.

When I passed my state boards, he snuck into the nurse's lounge and wrote on the blackboard.

"Congratulations Fran, RN!"

He sent flowers and candy to me at work. Once, on the day shift, he brought a candle in to the cafeteria and lit it for our lunch. I was blushing. Everyone in the hospital seemed to know about us and he didn't try to keep it a secret.

We went for long walks. He was taking some black and white photography courses at Rochester Institute of Technology. The camera always came with us. We went to Highland Park, where the Lilac Festival happens every year. He took his typewriter along and wrote me poems. I have three boxes of them.

He was into health food and always shopped at the local natural food store. Soon his bulgur, beans, typewriter, and laundry were moving into my apartment. I called his laundry bag his cowboy bag because it was made from a children's novelty fabric with little cowboys printed on it.

He was still waiting for his divorce to finalize. He knew I played the piano, so he decided we were going to rent a piano. I was ecstatic at the thought. I never even realized this was an option. When my parents came for a visit, he hid the cowboy bag and pretended we weren't living together. My mom admitted after we were married that she knew all along that we were cohabiting.

We didn't even have a couch. I had a chair that someone had given me. I sat on his lap, and we talked for hours. We arranged our work schedule so it was identical, and we wouldn't miss any time together. Frequently after working all night, we'd go out for breakfast with a group of people from work. We had a great time cutting our own tree for our first Christmas together, dragging it home, and decorating it. I had a little television. It was an odd one, with an aqua colored front. We would put it on the living room floor and sit there to watch football. Eventually we got a couch. It wasn't brand new, but we were excited to have it.

He took me to Letchworth Park. We loved to go hiking. It was beautiful. It had a reputation of being the Grand Canyon of the East. Mr. Romantic carved our names inside of a heart on a tree. Little noticeable things were happening. An apple baked in the heat of our dashboard. A daisy that we had plucked and put into a glass of water sprouted roots. The forecast for our first date was rain, but instead it became a beautiful sunny day. We attributed these as signs that we were meant to be. At Letchworth, he sat me down and started to tell me about the Mormon religion and how much it was a part of his life. I was already prepared. I had anticipated this and read a book about it prior to our trip. I told him I would visit his church. I went to the church, as promised, and almost joined. I admired their family values. My brother in Saratoga was diligently praying for me. I never joined that church. Our courtship was a fun season in our life. He asked me to marry him but that was easier said than done.

Chapter 2:
Dreamers

It was May 27, 1978. Flags flew and campers crawled along the interstate. Widows of veterans mourned. My Ohio relatives stopped to change their clothes in the cemetery. The perfect day had finally arrived. We had gone through all the obstacles, ridden emotional roller coasters, and broken all the rules to get to this day. We stole Memorial Day weekend for our wedding. My girlhood wedding dreams were coming to pass, complete with yellow roses and Lily of the Valley for my bouquet.

The time leading up to that day was challenging. Three months prior, we had chosen the date and drove to my hometown to make the plans. We booked the Old Stone Mill in Skaneateles for the reception and hired the band. We ordered the flowers and invitations with the date of May 27. There was one glitch. Phil's divorce was not yet complete. Everyone was holding their breath. Some might say we made all those preparations in blind faith. Others might say, and did say, that we were rebellious and bullheaded. Then, on May 17, ten days prior to the set wedding date, Phil's lawyer handed him the divorce papers. We went from one end of the counter in Monroe County for him to sign them, and to the other end to get our marriage license. The lawyer and his secretary had an argument. She accused him of expediting a divorce when the groom-to-be was still on the rebound. She quit her job and walked out on the attorney.

My mother was livid. This left her no time to make the gown for her first daughter's wedding. My new niece would only be a month old, and my sister was trying to cope with being a new mother. Grandpa was having another severe attack of the gout. None of this mattered to us. We were convinced our love could conquer everything. We believed that not even death could separate us. We were invincible.

No one was going to squelch this special love we had found. One day, I walked into the unit at work and found a bouquet of flowers and a box of candy waiting for me. My fiancé was a real charmer. We arranged our vacations and made our plans. Our honeymoon in New Orleans was going to come to pass. The rushing began.

Suits and gowns in Swedish colors of yellow and blue took their places in closets of the wedding party. Even though his parents were Danish immigrants, we had learned that there was also Swedish blood in the genes. We stenciled over a hundred tapered white candles with our names and the wedding date. Those were our chosen wedding favors. The white napkins were etched with the words, "Thank you for sharing our joy."

The day before the wedding my mother took me to pick up the gown. The seamstress who was attaching the yellow flower appliqués had gone to New York City for a family funeral. The gown wasn't ready. Then the florist announced that he couldn't find any real Lily of the Valley, so he'd placed silk ones in the bouquet. My mom knew my dream of having those flowers in my bouquet. She wouldn't settle for fake ones.

After we got home, she went up and down the main street of our little town, seeking, and finding the real thing. Neighbors donated to my bouquet.

We scurried from one task to another that day in my sister's Pinto. It began to stink. First, we attributed this to the possibility that my brother had stuffed Limburger cheese up the tailpipe. We stopped at a service station and

14

found out that the battery cell had gone completely dry. Soon we were back on the road, thankful that nothing worse had happened to the car. I realized that my garter was missing. Mom pulled over. I went out in traffic looking for my something blue along the roadside. The search was in vain. I returned to the car, frustrated and slightly depressed. Everything seemed to be going wrong. Glancing into the back seat, I saw it. There, on the floor, was the neatly packaged lacy garter, staring spitefully back as if laughing at my circumstances. I had forgotten about putting it on the roof and apparently it blew back in when we began to drive. At the end of the day, another woman finished my gown. Phil was about to arrive at my girlfriend's home just in time to get ready for the rehearsal party.

Guests began arriving from out of town. We drove the seven miles to the church from my parent's and went through the music and vows we had written to each other. At the restaurant later, the famished frolicking group enjoyed a delicious meal. Then it was time to tip the waitress. Tipping was one thing my fiancé believed in. He even tipped gas station attendants. I didn't like it when he decided to place the tip in the back pocket of the waitress's tight leather skirt. Jealousy won and the war began. I was fuming. We took the argument outside near the phone booth. We were both screaming. I was crying. We left the party, angry at each other. I wasn't sure until the phone call the next morning if the wedding was still on. When I heard the words "I love you" spoken to me in Vietnamese I knew I could start getting ready. The wedding was scheduled for noon. Phil was so nervous that he rose too early and dressed in his wedding suit. He showed up at the breakfast table at my girlfriend's house. He was ready to go but it was four hours too early.

The dream was coming true. Everything came together like a symphony. During the ceremony, my sister played our favorite song, "Evergreen" on her flute. My brother sang "The Wedding Song," We read the vows we had written to each other. It was a picture-perfect day. The trees were full of pink blossoms. Photos were taken with the lake in the background. People on the street and in the park lined up with "Oohs" and "Ahh's" while the wedding party posed. Later, the photographer said that he liked one of the pictures so much that he used it in his advertising.

Inside the reception area, the band played on. It was the hottest day of the year up to that point. The air conditioner broke. The waitress spilled wine on my father-in law and my grandfather. My father-in-law remained the staunch Lutheran that he was and didn't drink. He was a bit disgruntled. I begged him to dance with me. This was another tradition he didn't favor. He held his ground and only managed to get through one dance with my mother-in-law, biting his lip while he danced.

We passed the traditional Italian wedding cookie tray and danced the Tarantella. We would be together then and always. Our lives would be evergreen and forever, just like the song. After the reception, we waved good-bye to our guests and got in Phil's little white Mazda to begin our drive south to New Orleans.

The coming months brought new trials. Only two months into the marriage, our love was put to the test. Too soon, life began to take an unexpected turn. This life would prove if our undoubting love was made to survive.

Chapter 3:
Broken Ones

I asked God to send me someone to love. Little did I know at the time what challenges I would face. I began to see there was an invisible wall somewhere in my husband's heart that no one could break through. Only two months into our marriage, Phil wanted to have a Vietnamese boat person, as they were referred to, come and live with us. He thought that we could get a student to move in. It had been two years since the fall of Saigon. We saw images on television of the helicopters leaving the ground. People were hanging from the choppers, trying to escape the communists who were taking over. All Phil had told me about his involvement in the Army was that he had been a medic with the First Cavalry, 8th Engineers for a thirteen-month deployment that began in 1968. I was only fifteen in 1969. Woodstock was happening in the southern part of the state. I remembered how sad I felt when Walter Cronkite announced the body count at the end of every evening newscast. I didn't understand why he was so insistent on having someone move in with us so soon after our wedding. It became the main source of contention between us.

Years later, looking back, I can still picture the argument that took place less than six months after our wedding. It plays like a movie. I watch the scenes replay in my mind, like a nightmarish broken record. I watch the man and woman, engaged in another nonsensical verbal volleyball. Once again, a minor disagreement escalates into a full-scale eruption. Angry words transform into pleading begs for understanding as the voices of the broken ones grow in crescendo. Attempts to gain understanding die in vain. Words, transformed into harsh syllables, wield indelible wounds into the hearts. Futility grows as the invisible wall goes up between them, justifiably built with the bricks of hurt that they hurl at each other. As sudden as a blinding winter squall, coldness permeates the air.

"I don't care," he states, and focuses his empty gaze onto the ceiling. From the place where he lays supine on their bed, his countenance instantly changes from contentious and twisted, from numb to indifferent. His eyes follow the sliver of light that filters through the curtain in the pre-dawn hours of that day. She screams out.

"I don't understand why you won't answer me! You're so cold and mean! What's the matter with you?" Like the crack of a gunshot ringing through the crisp night air, her railing accusation pierces the wounded husband on his bed. Carried on the vector of revenge, the words fall on deaf ears. He lies still. She feels ignored and unimportant. Frustration mounts. Why can't he understand why she doesn't want a Vietnamese boat person to come and live with them? They have only been married for two months. Finding no place to hide, emotions from her broken heart erupt into a barrage of words like the finale at a fireworks display.

He lies still, like a stone, impervious to further malice, unbendable, and unwilling to give or forgive. He has withdrawn, like a wounded animal retreating to lick his wounds. The light on the ceiling beckons his attention and lulls him into the comfort of isolation. The warm place of refuge on the mattress offers complacency. His obvious indifference has now drawn the line of separation between them. Tasting the salt of hot tears flowing down her cheeks, she acknowledges his immovable, heartless posture and leaves the room. Moving down the dark stairway, she is sobbing like she has never known. Her heart has been vulnerably exposed and trampled, left to its fate by the nonchalant one who lies, frozen emotionally, upstairs. Where is the promise of his comfort? Where is his shoulder now? Only months had gone into this marriage. Where was the love and companionship? Why was she left so alone? "How could he be so cold?" The questions flood her mind, driving her to retrieve the wedding album for answers. Trying to gain control of her racking shoulders, she opens the brown leather book. Swollen eyes try to focus on the page before her. Tears have blurred the place where her smile gazes back. In that reflection, she is looking into a whole new world. It will send their lives careening for much of the future. That world, in which abides the wife of this Vietnam veteran, already has her in its grasp. The pain was only beginning.

Chapter 4:
A Stranger Moves In

In the months to follow, I left my job at Strong Memorial Hospital. In the ICU I became interested in neurology, and later transferred to the rehabilitation unit so I could follow some of the patients from their trauma through the rehab process.

My time was devoted to sleepy mornings getting Phil off to work. I awoke slowly with my cup of coffee and the company of the Phil Donahue show. Soon I was pregnant. I crocheted a sweater set for my new baby. Afternoons were spent in the sun. I dreamt of which delicacy I could cook up to surprise my husband when he came home from work. From time to time I took short job assignments. This included working in critical care units in hospitals all over Rochester. I ended up finding a job at the state psychiatric center. My strong stomach couldn't hold up to some of the conditions in that institution. Patients were often left in their beds, contracted in fetal positions for years, and fed pureed brown and green meals. Staff took their places in the solarium alongside those who were privileged enough to be wheeled out to the room. They watched the afternoon soap operas before ending their shift. I frequently visited the bathroom, heaving, before finally quitting. From there, I went to work as a front desk receptionist at an insurance company.

Shortly thereafter, Phil quit his job as a respiratory technician and went to volunteer at a community advocacy group. He said he always wanted to work in the field of social work. He believed in helping the underdog, and I believed in him, so I encouraged him that he could do anything he wanted. He also believed in the "Robin Hood" theory of living. He got upset over every social injustice he heard or read about. I didn't know that in the days ahead, this would become an obsession with him.

While volunteering, an opportunity led him to a job as a paralegal at a place called *Veteran's Outreach Project*. He had never done paralegal work before. Since he was a veteran who cared about making a change for others, he was their man. Phil always told me that there were two kinds of people in the world-those who made the news and those who read the news. He said he wanted to be a newsmaker. They offered him a salary and an office. He was to interview the vets that came into his office and prepare their cases in attempts to get their discharges upgraded. He would then have to research their military records and prepare a legal brief in their behalf. It would be submitted to the Board of Veteran's Appeals for the final decision. After that, hopefully, the discharges could be upgraded, enabling them to get benefits.

At the time, there was no mention of memories or details from the war. He did tell me he was there at the time of TET offensive, which was the Vietnamese New Year. He seemed to have made a perfect adjustment from the jungles of Pleiku and Song Be to the ice cream shops of Oakland, California. It appeared that he loved his job. He would come home and tell me the stories of other veterans who came to his office. He was frustrated when military records were missing. Regardless of the frustration, he liked the challenge. He began coming home later, working long hours on his new mission of helping his brother vets. He had a new cause. When the advocacy work paid off and he won a case for another vet, he was thrilled. I just kept going with my new days of pregnancy and planning apple pies and surprises for my hard-working husband.

The day came when Phil decided that we would make a great medical team in the refugee camps of Thailand. The war had ended three years prior, but there were still many people that needed help.

"I have no interest in going to Thailand." I told him.

"If I wanted to do that, I would have joined the Peace Corps."

He repeatedly tried to persuade me to go and I repeatedly refused. There were too many arguments. We started going to a marriage counselor. Not long after that, the news overflowed with stories about the boat people and the refugee camps. More arguments ensued. One morning we went for a walk in the circle around our townhouse and he sat me down on the park bench, proclaiming that he had decided.

"I've decided that we're going to go work in one of those refugee camps."

I jumped off the bench, losing my temper and proclaiming that I would not go. One way or another, he was determined we were going. We didn't.

I couldn't understand his sudden change in focus from us to the issues of Vietnam. On top of this, I was threatened that I was going to lose him to another woman. I felt inept, not being able to be the person he wanted me to be and go off to Thailand with him. Between my irrational fears and his growing fixation on Vietnam, along with the stress of his job, tensions were rising. The anticipation of a major change as new parents didn't help. What I didn't know then, and found out months later, was that his suppressed memories of Vietnam ten years prior were beginning to surface. While I was home planning the next meal, he was at his office listening to the testimonials of the vets. He didn't tell me until a few months later, that after some of them left his office, he would sit and hurl books from his desk to the wall at the far end of the room in a rage that was only starting to boil.

Phil was given an opportunity to present some cases before the Board of Veteran's Appeals at the World Trade Center in New York City. Trip expenses would be paid, and we decided to stay with his sister in Brooklyn. She was a registered nurse from Denmark. Ella and I always got into shop talk. She was quite a bit older than I, but we could talk about anything. I loved going to New York with Phil. Brooklyn was his hometown. He took me to see his old neighborhoods. Bay Ridge, Ocean Ave, and others were where he had lived. We walked down streets past brownstone houses and into the delis that sold pumpernickel, mackerel, and cheeses that he had grown up on. He took me to Coney Island and told me stories about the times he and his father would walk down to the Narrows to look at the boats. Life was never complete without our purchase of New York pizza and Italian ice.

We heard there was a new movie out that had to do with Vietnam and he wanted to see it. We went to an old theatre in downtown Manhattan to watch "The Deer Hunter." Phil watched intently. In the darkness of the theatre, a foreboding feeling started to rise within me. Suddenly, in the middle of the movie, Phil stood up and started crying hysterically.

"There's part of me in there!"

I couldn't make out the other unintelligible words he cried before he sat back down. I was at a loss of what to do about this. I wanted the floor to swallow me. Strangely, no one said anything or tried to kick us out. Phil calmed down.

We watched the rest of the movie, and then drove back to the apartment in silence. I tried to figure out why this was happening with my husband. The episode wasn't discussed and when his assignment was finished, we went back to Rochester and prepared for the coming of our baby.

We began going to classes on natural childbirth. Everything was going smoothly. One night, Phil grew impatient with me about some trivial matter. He became angry and told me he wasn't going to the classes with me anymore. All I did was cry. I didn't understand why he seemed to be abandoning me and I certainly didn't understand his sudden moodiness. Once, during a local trip on the main route around Rochester, another senseless argument erupted. It escalated until he stopped the car and decided that he was going to walk home. It didn't matter to him that I was pregnant and scared of his behavior. He refused to get back in the car and I drove home alone.

We decided to move to Syracuse before the baby came. We would be closer to both sets of grandparents. Mine were twenty minutes from the city and his were near Oneonta, two hours away. With the help of his coworkers, we packed up everything in our townhouse and moved to a basement apartment on the East side of Syracuse. Occasionally we would go to Rochester for his visitation weekend with his three children. His former wife distrusted him and plenty of emotional baggage always accompanied the visit.

Days passed quickly with baby plans. Phil still didn't have a job. He found out that the Red Cross had a small program doing the same kind of work he had done for the vets in Rochester. There were only two people doing that job in Syracuse, even though the needs were far greater for veteran's advocacy. With the encouragement of the Red

Cross, he wrote a grant. He worked long and hard on this, doing research to prove there were many vets who needed the help. It was denied, so there would be no job. They didn't have the funds to pay his salary.

After that, he worked for a diaper delivery service. He had to quit because he developed a bad rash on his legs. The doctors cited it as unknown and unusual. This was not the standard contact dermatitis. We wondered if Agent Orange had anything to do with this. Many vets were experiencing strange rashes that were attributed to the dioxin in Agent Orange.

In his idle time, Phil began to read the *New York Times* on a regular basis. He was attracted to every social injustice he found. He became obsessive about filling folders with clippings concerning those injustices. He told me continually that he believed in fighting for those less fortunate who were not being given the benefit of the doubt. Vietnam was springing up in the news everywhere, as well as in our lives. It was 1979. Ten years prior, he had been there. It was the ten-year anniversary of the TET offensive. Pictures and articles inundated magazines, newspapers, and television. He began cutting out pictures of soldiers in Vietnam and posting them around our apartment.

"This is a part of me." He reminded me, creating a reason that he should be doing this.

Occasionally, he'd say a tiny thing about his experience as a medic. I tried understanding but felt that my understanding was falling way too short. Near the third trimester of my pregnancy, every time I walked out of the bathroom, I stared into the hollow, gaunt gaze of a battle-weary soldier. From the black and white photo, that soldier made eye contact with me from under his helmet. The hollow stare made me feel uneasy. Phil refused to remove it.

I was beginning to get spooked by all this Vietnam stuff. I was naive about it all and I just wanted a normal life, whatever that was. Arguments were occurring more regularly. There was a police helicopter that routinely flew over our apartment every night. If Phil was reading the paper when it flew overhead, he'd instantaneously drop the paper and grab his imaginary M-16. I began to have nightmares of helicopters. If anyone came up suddenly upon him and startled him, he would automatically respond in a self-defensive stance. Sometimes, his flailing arm would hit people, who were always gracious about it, much to my amazement. Things were escalating. The media wasn't helping our personal life. I wished it would all go away.

Then came the next movie, "Apocalypse Now." I felt I had to go to watch it to somehow protect him. That movie only made things worse. There was a sense of darkness I never knew pervading our lives. It only intensified. Back home, Phil decided to add his artwork to the bamboo screen that hung between the kitchen and living room. I didn't mind the oriental letters. It was the drawing of the little hangman that bothered me. He offered no explanation about it. His long hours of being withdrawn and lying on the couch in the dark, began to frighten me more. There didn't seem to be anything to pull him out of this. Even proclaiming to him how much I loved him wouldn't ease the reality we were living with. On a regular basis we would hear of another Vietnam veteran who took his own life.

We heard that Ella was coming up to visit my in-laws. She was turning fifty and there was going to be a birthday dinner at a restaurant. Phil's whole family would be there. I began to look forward to the change of environment. He still didn't have a job, the baby was due in a month, and we didn't know what the future held. He was under a lot of stress as head of the household. We went to the birthday party dinner on September 23, 1979. It was sixteen months since our wedding in May of 1978 and ten years since Vietnam. Everybody was happy to see each other. It was always great to be with Ella and I was glad to get away from the nightly helicopter ritual.

Phil, unlike many, had not been a drinker or into drugs when he was in the war. That night he had several glasses of wine with his dinner. He needed to unwind from all the stress he was under. The party progressed from the restaurant to my in-law's house. There, he began drinking Scotch. The amazing thing was that he wasn't getting sick. When it was time to go, my brother-in-law had to argue with Phil to let me drive the car on the dirt roads back to his sister's log cabin where we were staying. Being pregnant, I had not been drinking. The hours ahead held a new kind of terror. We didn't know it, but the adversity before us was propelling us right into the hands of God.

Chapter 5:
Night of Fear

After much persuasion, my brother-in-law persuaded Phil to let me take the wheel. The car bounced over the rugged dirt road en-route to my sister-in-law's cabin in the woods. I wondered what the baby, now eight months old in my womb, was thinking of this bumpy escapade. It was late, somewhere after midnight, and the road grew narrower as we progressed. Tall grass closed in on us on both sides. The smell of alcohol hung in the air like a bad memory. Regardless of the cold September night, I wanted to open the window. My thoughts were quickly pushed aside when my husband started to be actively alarmed. Without warning, he began to yell at me.

"Hit the lights! Lay Low! Charlie's out there!" Simultaneous with his yelling, he began to hit the dashboard. He hit it so hard that he cracked it. The sound of his hand smashing into it every time made me wonder what he would destroy next in his frenetic state of mind.

I tried to rationalize. We had been under all that stress. His Mazda had even been repossessed because we couldn't come up with twenty dollars. They came in the night and took it away. The intrusive memories of Vietnam had become part of every day. His frantic state continued to escalate. He seemed to be in a panic. I tried to used reality orientation. This always worked with elderly people who had straying minds and wandered off on unrelated topics in their conversations.

"Phil, we're in a car going to your sister's. We just left the birthday party for Ella." This was all done in vain. He kept banging the dash.

"Stop the jeep!" He yelled. Desperate tones emanated from him as he shouted his demand. I turned the radio on, thinking the reality of music would stop him. It didn't.

"Charlie's out there!" he cried out hysterically.

Driving the Malibu further into the darkness, I realized that this must be a flashback. I tried to talk to him to distract him.

"Come on, Phil, you had too much to drink. We are going to your sister's house. We are in New York, not Vietnam."

None of my words deterred him. At that moment, to him, the cornfield was elephant grass in the jungle, and we were in a jeep surrounded by the enemy. Fear clutched me as I drove, eager to get to that house. I prayed that they had arrived home from the party before us. The trees along the road blackened. Their branches lured us like groping tentacles, pulling us closer to the tall grass where Phil believed the enemy was. The dank smell of Autumn's rotting leaves hung in the air. Threatening thoughts filled my mind.

"He acts as if he doesn't even know me. I had heard some of these stories in the news lately. Will he suddenly think I am his enemy?"

Phil's bizarre motions grew more desperate with each passing second as the invisible Viet Cong approached. If he could have made us disappear, he would have. Would he grab the wheel? Would he jump out of the car? Would he grab me if I didn't comply with his demands? The presence of this stranger in my car gave me more angst and confusion. I thought of the baby and prayed under my breath. No one was on this road but the trees, elephant grass, the enemy, and us. Waves of nausea flooded me as I drove. Every intense moment lasted too long. I tried to focus. My arms began to shiver, and a chill crawled slowly from my hands on the steering wheel and up to my shoulders. My chest was pounding. At the same time, it felt like the blood was draining from my head. I felt faint. How would anyone find us here if he decided I was the enemy? His strength frightened me, as if he was a giant, and I, a mere ant. Realizing that I was the only one in control, I pushed on trying to suppress the frightening thoughts.

"Hit the lights!" He demanded again. His voice was more anxious. The irritated urgency in his tone told me that this couldn't go on much longer. A man in fear must conquer that fear to survive. I reached out to touch his arm, hoping it would calm him. His muscles were taut and hard as concrete. His eyes were fixed on the field beside us. The unknown gripped me just when the sight of the driveway came into view.

Upon arriving and seeing lights on, I felt relief. Help was surely near in the form of my brother-in-law. My sister-in-law came to the basement door.

"Hurry! Get your husband!" I yelled. She went in and returned quickly. Approaching the car, she informed me,

"He's passed out on the bed. I can't get him up. What's wrong?"

By this time, Phil was already out of the car, crawling combat-style in his beige suit pants through the muddy yard, rock in hand. Apparently, the rock was needed to silence the barking dog that was tied near his doghouse. The VC couldn't be allowed to hear that noise. My husband was transformed into a soldier that night, defending himself from the invisible enemy as we watched without knowing what to do, or what came next. His sister had a brainstorm. She called out to Phil.

"Hey Phil! Do you want some popcorn?" Phil acted like he didn't know either one of us.

"Phil, this is your sister! We're at her house. Let's go in."

We began walking and he followed. Immediately after entering the basement, my husband-turned-soldier began to give us orders to barricade the door and place the container of gasoline in front of it. His sister lured him with the popcorn, and he was distracted enough to get him upstairs away from the gasoline. Once upstairs, we began to show him pictures of his children. He didn't seem to know any of them. We told him the obvious. I was pregnant. He thought it was great that it was his child, but didn't seem to know me, his wife. The calendar we showed him was accurately dated 1979 but he read 1969. He was paranoid about the adversary outside. Pacing about the room, he retrieved a cigarette from the counter and then found his way to the gun rack on the wall. Taking one gun from the rack, he aimed it out the window towards the invisible enemy.

"Lay down on the floor!" He commanded us. It was then that the baby pressing on my bladder summoned. I made a move to go to the bathroom. He stopped me.

"I need to go to the bathroom, Phil. You know, the baby keeps me going."

"Okay. You need to go to the head? Go on." He retorted briskly.

I was relieved to hear that the guns on the rack weren't loaded. I held my breath at the thought of Phil wandering upstairs to the gunroom and prayed that it wouldn't happen.

I can't remember how we got to the phone that night, but someone managed to call the ambulance. They showed up much later and told us the only thing they could do was take Phil to the VA hospital which was over an hour away. I bit my lip, hating the decision that rested with me. I was not willing to surrender my husband to more of the unknown that night. I decided if we just waited until he fell asleep, then he'd be okay after he got some rest. The paramedics left. The night wore on.

I listened to my heart pound in my chest and wondered how the night would end. My brother-in-law was still sound asleep. We were getting exhausted. We decided to call and wake up the other family members for help. Phil was wide awake, hyper-alert, and on-guard, making sure that Charlie wasn't going to invade this perimeter. Finally, after what seemed like a week of nights, my two other brothers-in-law cautiously approached the long dark driveway leading up to the log cabin. We had managed to sneak a call in to them. They entered the lower level and approached Phil under the guise that they were fellow soldiers. First, they convinced him that they were taking his place on guard duty that night, and then they played Vietnam with him.

"Phil, you need to get some sleep so you can take over in the morning. We'll take over so you can get some shut-eye."

Phil's nervous pacing continued as he talked with them, his voice heightened with intensity. He seemed to want to have some assurance. Pregnancy and suspense were squeezing the energy out of me. My hands were clammy, and I felt nauseated. Every cell screamed out for sleep. Finally, they persuaded him to lie down. After much pleading, he followed their instructions. The others stayed awake until he was asleep, then spent the next hours camped out in chairs. With much restlessness and tons of persuasion, my weary vet closed his eyes and slept. It was 5:30 am.

He woke with a start at eight o'clock and bolted upright as the morning sun greeted us all too soon. He gave me a morning kiss, and then began to inquire.

"Where is everybody?"

"Sleeping. It's been a long night."

"Why did I sleep with my clothes and shoes on?" I told him what happened. He wandered into the living room where the others were snoring in their places. He suggested we go for a walk. I shuddered when the cold air kissed my face. It helped to wake me up.

The country hills were beautiful that September morning. We could see for miles around as the morning mist began to lift. Except for the singing birds, the new day was quiescent as we walked up the dirt road. Exhaustion and tension walked up my spine. I began to shake inwardly, wondering what I would do if he went into another flashback. Approaching the dense trees, he wanted to go further in. I persuaded him we had to get back to the others who would be worried about us. I prayed that they'd wake up when we came in. They did. We put the coffee on while the men talked to Phil about the night. Before we left for our two-hour trip home that day, they had convinced him that we needed to seek psychiatric help for Phil. Bonded by this experience that would forever be a part of our memories, we said our good-byes and went home to our apartment. As we drove silently home, we knew that the unknown lurked ahead, waiting for us in Syracuse.

Chapter 6:
I Make a Way Where There is No Way

After the initial flashback and shortly before the baby was due, Phil was admitted to the psychiatric floor of a local hospital. I hated having him there as an inpatient. It was a beige, boring, and depressing place. The baby was due at any time. I packed my stuff and went over to stay at my parent's house, twenty miles away. I would stay there in case I went into labor. Crying myself to sleep at night became ritualistic. I was scared and wondered what the future would hold.

The baby turned in my uterus. It went into a frank breach position. That meant the head was up and the child could have been born with a prolapsed cord. It was two weeks past the due date. The day I found out that I'd most likely have to have a Cesarean I went to our apartment, rocked in the new wicker chair my sister gave me, hugged the teddy-bear I'd had since I was two, and cried. So much was going wrong. The baby was overdue. They told me there was only a two percent chance at thirty-eight weeks gestation that the baby would turn on its own. The doctors were talking about Phil not being allowed to be present because they feared the sight of blood might trigger a flashback. Everything we dreamt about was falling apart. I didn't know what would happen. I rocked and cried my eyes out.

Back at one of the initial meetings we met the psychiatrist, who himself was a Navy vet. He was from an earlier era and didn't seem to have much knowledge or, or give much credence to, the issues of PTSD. He mislabeled my husband as a schizophrenic, like many vets at that time were experiencing. Thorazine, an anti-psychotic drug, was prescribed, and he called the flashbacks "breaks with reality," which justified the false diagnosis. I remember Phil hiding the pills under his tongue and then spitting them out when the nurse left the room.

I visited him daily. He began to have a recurrent nightmare. He told me that in the nightmare, he saw a burning helicopter and men on fire. It haunted him to have this occur nightly. Little by little, through therapy and dreams, with memory finally kicking into gear, the story came out. He trembled as it poured out of him. He was at the field hospital in Chu Lai. A fever and sickness had made him an inpatient there. At first, they thought he might have malaria, but decided it was pneumonia. Wheezing, crackling lung sounds, high fevers, and bodily aches were the symptoms that overlapped the two diagnoses. The enemy had gotten between the green and red wires that delineated the perimeters. All patients that were able had to take their weapon and go through a tunnel under the hospital to defend the others. An American chinook had gotten shot down. There were men on it burning and screaming. Phil remembered shooting one of them. He knew they were going to die. He remembered the fiery crash and the screams.

The next bit of memory forced itself to the surface. He remembered seeing the shoes of the commander as he circled him in the tent, barraging him with questions about who gave the orders to shoot. When combined with the recollection of the first incident, it became clear that he had been involved in a tragic occurrence. He had suppressed that memory for years and it finally came forth in all its ugly, painful ways. Years later, we learned that he had received the Army Commendation medal for what occurred that night. Strangely, the reasoning for it was not in his records, but we had a citation from when he received the medal. It stated that he had acted with heroic measures on the day of the incident. After making his way down the hospital floor one night doing the combat crawl in another flashback, and several more sessions of therapy, he was discharged.

As it turned out, the baby came two weeks after her due date. She fell into the two percent range and flipped to the right position, so I was able to go through with the. natural childbirth. Phil was allowed to be there, without any problems occurring. Tanya was born November tenth. She was a little rose to me. She had glowing red cheeks and lots of hair. The nurses put a tiny mint green bow in her hair. She was perfect. She was a blessing in the middle of the turmoil.

Seventeen months later, Christopher was due. I went to the doctor and found out I was pregnant again. This time I had fallen into another two percent range and gotten pregnant with an intrauterine device. My nursing knowledge told me that I could have gone into septic shock being pregnant with the IUD. I came home crying and frightened. I thought something bad was going to happen to me. My doctor assured me that sometimes the babies got delivered holding the IUD in their hand.

Soon after I found out I as pregnant, we went to a bible study we had started attending. The woman of the house was pregnant. She said God had given her peace about it when she discovered the scripture in I Timothy 2:15.

"Women shall be preserved through the bearing of children if they continue with faith, love, sanctity, and self-restraint."

I grabbed onto that scripture like it was medicine. I printed it on paper and put it all over my apartment where I would see it. I memorized it and whenever I felt fear, I would say it out loud. Eventually, it got into my heart and spirit. I believed that the baby was going to be born without problems. I would be fine. Instead of fear I felt peace.

Many situations turned around while Phil was on his road to inner healing. It took plenty of trials to get to that place. We loved living in our apartment but with another baby on the way we needed more room. We didn't have much income. I began to pray about it. As I knelt at the couch and prayed, asking God how we could ever possibly afford a bigger place to live, I heard his still small voice, inaudible, but sure, in my heart.

"I make a way where there is no way."

The next day I was reading the evening paper. There was a bungalow with five bedrooms on a double city lot listed for sale for $16,000. I showed Phil and we decided to inquire. We told the woman our circumstances. She was willing to do a land contract with us which allowed us to pay her, and the deed would be in our name. Both of our sets of parents were able to give us a thousand dollars. We used it for a down payment. The payments were only one-hundred sixty-eight dollars per month.

The house was huge. The property was at the end of a city street. We thought it must have been the first farmhouse on the road years ago. It sat on a hill with stairs leading up to the front porch. The lot had many trees on it and there were yellow primroses crawling up the front. It was old but it was very livable. We dreamed of the day we might afford to remodel the huge place. We moved in before the baby was born. We were very happy. My Danish immigrant in-laws came to visit for a few days, and we had room for them to stay. I can still hear my father-in-law with his thick Danish accent calling for his wife from the porch.

"Marie, come out to the garden."

One morning that very hot and humid in July, while everyone was watching the royal wedding on television, Christopher made his entrance into the world. I was thrilled to meet my first son. Labor only lasted four hours, as opposed to the first one that lasted twenty hours. He was a joy and an encouragement to us all. I was so happy to have him.

Phil connected the front porch to the side porch. When our children got a little older, they would ride up and down from one end to the other on their big wheels. My sister gave us a black lab. We named her Mattie. Phil used to stand the dog up on its hind legs while, he, Tanya, and Chris held paws and hands and danced in a circle singing, "Ring around the Rosie." That dog got out of the yard and disappeared one day, never to be found again. We were sad about the loss.

Soon we got another dog that Tanya named "Judah." It was a German Shepherd mix. One day, Judah disappeared from our yard too. The next day we got a call from the dog catcher. He said they found the dog but wanted to talk to us first before they brought her home. Apparently, some juveniles had decided to spray red paint on the parked cars in the park area nearby. They saw our dog running around and decided to spray her too. When the dogcatcher took her out of the truck, she was no longer brown, but a lovely shade of red. Phil took her outside and bathed her to get the paint off. On the news that night they told of the vandalism in the area. We got to see our dog on TV. Red dog running. Now we had a dog who was the newsmaker.

There were difficult trying times in the four years we lived there as well. We were in the furnace of affliction and didn't know why. The older people at church loved our family and told us countless times that God had his hand on us and had a big work ahead of us. They said he was preparing us. That was what gave me the hope to keep going through it all.

Vietnam was still present in our lives. One night, we were sitting on our couch under the roof on the side porch. It was raining heavy. Our pet white rabbit was in the cage Phil had made for him, suspended off the side of the porch. The kids were asleep. We were having a spat about something and in my anxiety, I raised my voice. Suddenly, Phil was on top of me, his forearm planted firmly against my throat. It was very dark as the rain poured down. I could barely speak. When I did, I tried to say one word.

"Jesus" It came out in a strangulated whisper. As fast as it happened, Phil stood up, apologizing frantically.

"I'm sorry! I was in Vietnam and all I knew was that I had to silence you! I'm sorry!"

I knew about the monsoons in Vietnam that he had lived through. He had described walking through the wet jungle. I knew that he was reliving when he jumped on top of me to silence me. Strangely, all I felt for him was forgiveness and pity. I didn't feel afraid even though I knew he could have killed me if he had kept that arm on my throat. We carried on with life.

Phil became unemployed for a year and a half. We ended up having to go on welfare and food stamps. He would go to the window early in the morning and watch all the cars as the people drove off to work. It was demoralizing for him. I got a job at a community hospital when Chris was only four months old. I hated to do it. I just finished my orientation and was about to go to work as scheduled when I got a strange letter from the hospital terminating me. I didn't understand it. I obtained a lawyer when I discovered that they had made blatant lies about me. They stated that I failed to walk a patient when I was supposed to and some other nonsense that never took place. My lawyer investigated. He said I should just let it go because they were so nasty about it. He felt if I pushed any further, they would cause me to lose my license. The only thing I could think that would have caused that job loss was that I had left an evangelical tract in the conference room. It was religious discrimination based on that. I didn't press it. Besides, I didn't like taking my babies to the sitter and going away while my husband was home going through hell. Ironically, I got a job with that hospital years later.

Phil had night sweats. He slept with his combat knife under our mattress. On Independence Day, I ran around the house turning on every fan and noisy apparatus I could find to drown out the sound of cherry bombs and firecrackers. The sound of those triggered flashbacks. We could never take the children to fireworks. The noise and lights reminded him too much of the flares and the tracers.

He took off several times. I would get the kids to bed and start to pray about where he might have gone. I couldn't leave the kids alone and go look for him. One night he went to a local bar. He had never been a perpetual drinker. I didn't know where he was. I found myself praying that he would become repulsed with whatever he was drinking. He finally came home. He said he had been at the bar down at the plaza, and suddenly he got sick of the alcohol and just couldn't stand to take another sip of it, so he came home.

Often, he would go away, and I asked God the same question.

"Where is he this time? North, south, east or west?"

It was routine for me to call the prayer chain and tell them he was gone again. There was a big group of people praying for him every time.

When Phil's father passed away in 1983, I was the one to have to tell him. He came home from work exhausted. When I broke the news, he got a startled, numb look in his tired eyes. His next step was out the door. He fled into the darkness of the night. I found him huddled in the back yard crying. This was the first person close to him that he had lost since Vietnam. I quietly and prayerfully supported him as we made our way through the funeral proceedings.

We had a sign on our porch. It said, "Jesus never fails." That sign was up and down. Whenever we had an argument, one of us would get mad and take the sign down and throw it. Then it would go up again later. We were still going to the church that our friends from New York pastored. The people kept assuring us that God had a purpose for us. One wise older lady repeatedly told us what she thought.

"God told me to tell you that you have so much. You have each other and your children."

So many things happened. Amid everything, it was sometimes hard to believe that God was really working. Many times, God divulged to me the plans that Phil had concocted to leave again. On one such occasion, an uneasy, suspicious feeling arose within me. This had happened at the previous apartment whenever something was stirring with him. I was prompted to go to the backroom of our huge old house. It was there that I found the packed green Army knapsack. It smelled like dirt. I opened it. There were various items needed for survival. That combat knife was in the bag. There was a note with a list of things to pack. The heading on the note was in bold letters.

"Use deception at all times." That was one of the last straws for me. I confronted him with his deception. This time I was begging him to leave. I couldn't take it anymore. He refused to leave, and I wasn't sure how we could go on with that deception hanging over our heads. I felt understandably insecure.

Winter came. We had been to Rochester for Phil's visitation with his children. The cold evening gave birth to a new blanket of snow. Our trip home had been a grueling one, full of contention. It was nearing Christmas and our pocketbooks were empty. We had our two small children, but unemployment and financial burdens had mounted to an unbearable level, making gift-buying something out of our realm. Once home, physically and emotionally exhausted, we were on our way to bed at ten o'clock. The phone rang. It was our Pastor.

"I'd like to come over for a visit, if possible."

As tired as we were, we'd never turn down a visit from this shepherd that we loved. A sense of expectation filled the air. We wondered why he wanted to come here so late at night. The children were tucked into bed when the Pastor showed up at the door. He came directly to the kitchen and began his explanation.

"There is a man in Dallas, Texas that helps a needy family every Christmas. His brother goes to a local church, and he heard about your need. He wants you to have this."

Extending his hand, my husband gingerly took the envelope that was offered him. Once again, God had chosen to bless us despite us. The handwritten testimony brought tears to our eyes as the one-hundred-dollar bill fell to the floor. This stranger told us how he had grown up poor, on the streets of New Jersey, and had made a promise to God as he surrendered his life to Him. If God blessed him and helped him, he would do the same for someone every year. He had chosen us. In addition, there were bags full of gifts for the children. There were name brand clothes and toys. There was a beautiful dress for Tanya with velvet, ribbons and lace and a jumpsuit for Chris. There was a stuffed Snoopy doll and a bunny rabbit doll wearing a watch with pockets for his keys and glasses on his nose. The Pastor moved to the porch momentarily and brought back a tyke bike in colors of pink and blue, perfect for our little girl.

God truly humbled us with this blessing for our children, as well as the blessing of knowing with more assurance than ever, that He can supply all our needs. The assurance that he gave us through this blessing could not be measured in money. The lesson learned was more than the gifts themselves. We were beginning to learn about God's way of humbling us.

That was not the end of it. A few mornings later, I stepped out onto our front porch and found gifts for the children at my feet. They were from a girl's club of a local church. The Christmas that we thought would be barren yielded much fruit from the loving kindness of the Lord.

There was a time when Phil drove the church bus. We all rode on it. We picked up kids from the inner city and brought them to church and back, singing all the way. Then he got a job as a school bus driver. After a while, he decided he didn't want to go to church with me and the kids anymore. He found every excuse possible to get out of going. Conveniently, the bus company needed a driver to take scouts up to the Adirondacks on a regular weekend basis. Of course, he did it. I diligently continued to go to church with my children. We were going to a different church at that time. Our beloved pastor friends from the first church had been called to start a new church in another place in New York State. We went to another church that was filled with life. That didn't change, even when Phil decided to stop going.

During that time, Phil decided to escape back to Vietnam. I found him sitting in the dark living room listening to depressing music from the sixties. He was reading every book that involved the Vietnam experience that he could get his hands on. He started smoking Pall Mall cigarettes just like he did over there. When men from the church and fellow vets would come to talk to him, he would make excuses not to see them. I was totally frustrated and at my wits end about how to help.

I used to visit an elderly lady, Rose, who had been a Christian for many years. She had a lot of wisdom. She loved our family and she had worked for many years at Teen Challenge. She was the one who taught me that when I was feeling hopeless, I could just say the name of Jesus repeatedly and He would be there for me. She also decided that Phil needed lots of prayer and a baptism of love to get the revelation of God's love for him. She was mightily used by God to hold me together at the time when I might have otherwise not been able to stand. I clung to the hope that God would turn the situation around.

Phil agreed to go with me to visit a church in the area that had a guest speaker. There was a prophecy spoken over us.

"For every step backward, God will take you two steps forward."

The tide slowly began to turn. I was constantly praying for renewal. We met a very loving, mighty man of God who was having revival meetings. To us, he was Brother Patton. He preached that the most important school Christians needed to attend was the "School of Knee-ology." When Phil and I went forward for prayer, he laid his hands on us to pray and we felt the power of God as we fell to the floor under the influence of that power, side by side. Doubters would say he pushed us down. I would venture to say that they have never experienced such a power.

Phil went to see Brother Patton. God used him mightily. Phil was delivered from those Pall Malls, throwing the last of them out the window own the way home and never touching them or any other cigarettes again. We heard that our friend had kidney problems. Later we heard that he had succumbed to kidney failure. He was only in his forties. We also heard that one of his roommates in the hospital had gotten healed under his ministry. We were thankful to be a part of his life.

I had a dream one night. I drew a picture of it when I woke up. It lined up with what we had been told a few years prior by the doctor. God showed me that Phil was like a boiling pot of water. He showed me that the pot was shaking from the pressure. I saw the shaking lid and steam escaping. He told me that Phil was like that pot, full of pressure that had to be let out slowly, and that he was healing him of the Vietnam problems. I began to get glimpses of hope for the return of the Prodigal son. First, I had seen it as a destroyed testimony. The dream showed me that the testimony was being strengthened.

Frequently, Phil would be gone, and I would have no idea where he went. I called people to pray. This was before cell phones were around.

"He's gone again. I don't know where he went this time."

In the beginning I would get a sitter and try to find him. On one occasion, when he left, he took our small amount of money and rented a red sports car. I had all I could do to hold it together emotionally until I got the kids tucked into bed. Then I lay, prostrate, on the floor, crying out to God.

"Which way did he go this time? Please turn him around and bring him home safely. Please let him hear Christian music somehow on his way home to remind him of who he is."

Hours later, Phil showed up. That time, he told me that he was on his way to the chemical plant in Ohio. He had done research on the people in charge and had gotten addresses of them all. He was headed out to seek retaliation for the Agent Orange issue. God intervened and turned him around. He came home down the New York State Thruway. He told me that he heard Christian music on the radio.

"It sounded like a chorus of angels singing as I drove home. No matter what station I tried to change it to, the same music kept playing." The awesome thing about this was that in those days there weren't loads of Christian music stations like there are today. I knew God was faithful to my prayers once again.

One morning, Phil was very despondent. At that time, he had a sales job, commission only, selling freezer plans. I saw him putting his shoes on to go somewhere.

"Where are you going?"

"I'm going out to knock on doors to get some sales so we can have some money." Little Tanya pulled at him, wanted to be picked up. He wouldn't pick her up. The oppression was so thick you could have cut it with a knife.

"How will you make sales when you are so depressed? I think maybe you should stay home today." I was worried that he was going to go off and hurt himself. I was always worried about that. The news was full of this happening with the vets.

47

"I have to try." He responded.

"OK. Can you please try to be home by three o'clock?" I thought if he had a structure to the day it would help.

"Sure." I watched him and prayed as he headed off on foot.

The afternoon came quick. I was upstairs in the rocking chair nursing Christopher. Tanya was taking her nap. I realized, with an urgency in my spirit that it was three o'clock and he wasn't home. I put the baby down and went to call for help. I just knew Phil was in trouble. I couldn't go anywhere because our car was out of gas, and I had no money. I picked up the phone to call Diane, the closest one to me at our church. She was someone I knew I could trust. The phone was like a tree in the middle of a New York winter. Dead. We hadn't been able to afford the payment. They must have turned it off.

I cried out to God.

"Please send someone to help us! Phil needs help!"

Within fifteen minutes, Diane pulled up in front of my house. She came to the back door.

"What's wrong with Phil?" I cried.

"He's down at the Public Safety Building. The cops picked him up on the South side of the city. He was driving a stolen car. They said he was armed, and they can't find the gun. Those kids just got dismissed from school and they want to find it before the kids get it. He told the cops that he was driving around the city and just had to get home by three o'clock like he promised you. You need to get down there and get him to tell you where that gun is." I was somewhat in shock. Diane let me take her car and stayed and watched the kids.

Down at the jail, I met a female police officer. Ironically, Phil and I had just met her for the first time. We had dinner the night before with her and her husband at my uncle's house.

"Fran, Phil is in that room. We need you to talk to him about where the gun is. We can't find it and we don't want any kids to get it. Before you go in there, I'm warning you. He is not the same Phil he was last night. Do the best you can."

She led me to a small room and let me in. There was the same depressed, dejected spouse of mine that had left home earlier that day. He certainly wasn't any different to me.

"I didn't have a gun, Fran. I stole the car from a local dealer. I wasn't going to hurt anyone. I just wanted to get away. I was driving down route 481, thinking that I had to get home on time. The cops were nervous when I told them I'm a Vietnam vet. When they frisked me, they didn't even notice my wallet in my pocket. See?"

He threw his wallet out on the table. I tried to encourage him, assuring him that God would see us through this. They kept him in jail that night. When they took him in, handcuffed like a major criminal, they wouldn't even let me kiss him good-bye. The arraignment was scheduled for nine-thirty the next morning.

That morning was amazing! I felt the peace of God that passes all understanding. The circumstances were dire, and I had no answers. The Court house was bustling with activity, but I was somehow at peace, floating above the circumstances. It was surreal. Our Pastor was there. I went into the court, and they arraigned Phil, charging him with a felony-armed robbery. At one point, I tried to tell the judge that Phil was a Vietnam vet suffering from PTSD and that he had not taken the car with criminal intent to steal. It was the fight-flight response to the stress in his life. The judge ridiculed me with his reply.

"Well, maybe we can find some Vietnam vets who still think that stealing a car is illegal." I was angered by that comment. I felt like jumping up and giving him a piece of my mind, but I stifled it.

I can't remember what the bail was placed at, but my parents bailed him out, taking a risk and putting their property on the line in case he decided to skip out. Our Pastor said that to leave Phil in jail at any length of time would have been like sending him back to Vietnam. I agreed that would have been the wrong course to take. It was bad enough that Phil was facing four mandatory years at Jamesville Penitentiary. There was no recourse of a plea bargain due to the charge of robbery associated with the stolen car.

Of course, the whole incident hit the evening news, complete with pictures of the stolen red car. I had people calling me up with questions of all kinds. God must have given me the ability to be what our Pastor referred to as "velvet covered steel." His motto at the time was, "Keep your eye on the solution, not the problem."

I certainly had a chance in real life to apply these lessons. My prayer life became more desperate. Every night after the kids fell asleep, I would take the picture of Jesus off the wall and place it on the chair in front of me. I don't know why I did that, but it gave me assurance. There, on my knees, I would cry out to God and plead with him to intervene. I literally cried over and over.

"God, please don't let Phil have to go to jail." I didn't know how the situation could ever turn around. It certainly looked impossible.

One night, God got ahold of me when I was praying.

"Why are you praying in fear? You need to pray in faith."

The lights went on inside my head. Of course! How could I expect God to move from my place of fear? Fear wasn't faith and it is faith that pleases God. I was reminded that he is a rewarder of them who diligently seek him. I changed my prayer. I still cried out. I was praying to a different tune.

"Thank you, God, that Phil is not going to have to go to jail." My faith began to grow. I began to expect. Things started to change.

Soon thereafter, the district attorney changed hands. In the whole process, it was discovered that the car salesman who gave Phil the test drive in that car was a man on parole. This was his first job out of prison. When they drove to the gas station on Erie Boulevard and Geddes Street in Syracuse, the man got out of the car to check the tires for air. As he was getting the air hose, Phil drove off with the car.

They got to the truth of the matter quickly. The guy had lied about the presence of the gun because he didn't want to lose his job. The "armed" part of the robbery charges was dropped. Phil was now eligible for a plea bargain. He didn't want to take any plea bargain. To him, it was a matter of principle and they had done him wrong. It took persuading to make him see that it would be better for him and the family if he took the plea. He finally conceded and was handed a plea bargain of five years of probation. During that time, there would be no trips to New York City for us. He was forbidden to leave the county. According to the probationary terms, Phil was ordered "not to change place of residence or be away from home overnight without prior permission from the officer of probation, to obtain steady employment with no changes without consent, not associate with any one of questionable character while on parole, no drug use, remain in psychological treatment until discharged, and keep out of all trouble." That was April 28, 1982, and five years seemed like forever.

Phil got accepted for the job as director for a half-way house for people returning to the community after prison. It was a beautifully renovated Victorian home on the East side of Syracuse. He was diligent about his job. The non-profit organization was waiting for grant money. Phil was working long hours to get the place up and running. That was great, but he wasn't getting paid. He was, however, gaining an excellent reputation with some of the more prominent citizens of the community. The probation officer told us that if he got letters from some of the community, supporting him, it might look commendatory. His probation time might be shortened.

The letters began to come. One such letter alluded to Phil's character in his service to the ex-offenders.

"Many speak of him as a man with a heart to help others. He showed a balance of love, but not pity, authority, but still concern."

Two years from the beginning, on June 18, 1984, Phil received a letter from the same judge that had lacked understanding at the arraignment. It was entitled, "Honorable Discharge from Probation." It stated that Phil had made substantial progress toward becoming a law-abiding citizen and useful member of society, and no longer required close supervision. God had done it! Just as it indicated in Psalm 37, he was vindicated.

"God will vindicate you as the noon-day sun." His probation time had been cut in half and he was free.

There were other challenges during this time as well. One big issue was that of visitation with his three older children. It seemed like every time we were going through some major difficulty, a letter would arrive from his ex-wife. She lived in Rochester. She went to court and had him ordered to pay more money for child support. We simply did not have the money. The lawyer reminded him that back support was accruing as well. One hundred dollars per month was way beyond anything we could afford at the time. Phil was ordered to be in Monroe County court by a specific date. We didn't know what else to do but bring our case before the real judge. We prayed constantly, beseeching God for his mercy. Phil went to Rochester on the date of the court hearing as expected. His former wife never showed up. Due to her absence on the designated day, our lawyer informed Phil that the case had been thrown out of court. He was vindicated once again.

Chapter 7:
Vets For Christ Is Born

Eventually, Phil decided to start his own landscape business. While he drove away from the house his words trailed behind.

"Dirt man rides again!"

Away he would go, rain or shine, in the green Vega station wagon with the hole in the floor of the driver's side. We managed to get to church in it three times a week even though the floor was starting to fall through. Sometimes it felt like we had to put our feet through the floor to drive it, just like Fred and Wilma.

Phil would load all the old wooden handled shovels and hoes he owned into the back of this family car and drive off to the rich part of the county where the doctors and lawyers would pay premium prices to have him do his creative, meticulous landscaping on their property. The excellency of his work spread by word of mouth. He often told me the many things God would teach him while working with nature. It was as if he came home with a sermon whenever he worked all day. Even in the rain he would go. He loved the rain. He had gotten used to it in the monsoons. Now he didn't have to be afraid to be out in it. The rain was a way to stay cool and the ground cooperated better when it was wet. There were times he would take Christopher with him when he was young to help trim lilacs and other hardy duties. There were times he took all of us to rake my grandmother's leaves or clean the yard for one of my widowed patients.

Our faith was still growing through the trials. Every time there was a hurdle, we worked through it. Most of the time, it was with difficulty, but we managed to get over it. We didn't know how our financial situation was ever going to resolve. We even had trouble paying the $168 mortgage. The land contract holder was very gracious with us. I used to think she was an angel. She never threatened to kick us out and she worked with us while we were on welfare and food stamps during the time Phil couldn't work.

On November 23, 1984, our youngest child was born. He was three years younger than his brother. Now we had one girl and two boys. Michael weighed in at nine pounds, two ounces. We had a little port-a-crib on the main floor so he could be downstairs with us during the day. Tanya was upset at first because she said she wanted a little sister. They all loved each other, and eventually loved the playroom that we had for them in that house. They frequently made their debuts in the living room with all kinds of costumes they created.

One very rainy Memorial Day, at the age of four, Tanya went into the closet in their playroom and came out proclaiming that she had just gone into her prayer closet and God had met her there. Her life demonstrated that something had taken place. She would frequently speak some short statement that went directly to our hearts. Once, during a heated discussion, she stood in the middle of us and spoke.

"With God all things are possible." The bickering ended immediately.

The children grew and enjoyed the double lot we had. Chris spent hours in the sandbox creating all kinds of things and playing with little cars and trucks. The kiddie pool was always busy in the summer, including the time I joined the kids on a peculiarly hot day. The swing that Phil put up in the tree on the side yard was loved by them all.

It wasn't long before we started to hear of other Vietnam veterans that were donning their camouflage suits and leaving their families. Sometimes families knew where they were, sometimes they just disappeared. During his long period of unemployment, Phil had attended a rap group for Vietnam veterans at the VA hospital. They met on Thursdays. It helped him to share with other combat vets. I also learned that I didn't dare inquire about the discussions in the group. It was off limits to me. The news was splendent with stories about vets going into rages and showing up with guns to destroy a place or person that irritated them. I was working per diem at University Medical Center, on a medical-surgical floor one day when I heard the other nurses complaining about a group of patients lately that were giving them difficulty. The complaints varied.

"Mr. D keeps sneaking cigarettes when he's been told not to smoke in here."

"That patient in room 16B closes his curtains all the time and doesn't associate with anyone he doesn't have to."

It occurred to me that these guys might be Vietnam vets. I checked the charts and found that they were similar ages. When I got bold and inquired of them and their families, I found that indeed they were. I saw that the nurses had no idea of why these guys were acting the way they were, or even who they were. I went to the nursing education department and asked if I could teach an in-service on PTSD on Vietnam veterans. They agreed. The class was full, and I could see that it had accomplished my purpose of raising the awareness of the vets with this problem in the hospital population. Some nurses from the veteran's hospital attended and soon I was asked to give the talk at the VA hospital. I thought that was a bit ironic.

They were the Veteran's Administration, and they were asking an outsider to come in and teach about the vets that they served daily. I taped Phil and another vet talking about their experiences in the war and returning home. I contacted the Vet Center and got a small video to show and passed out brochures on PTSD. The in-service was very well received.

Our burden for other veterans and families began to grow. Phil had the prompting to write a tract for veterans. He kept putting it off until one day he landed in the hospital with prostatitis. While he was recovering, he wrote his first tract, "Jesus Christ is my Point man." The tract was to explain to the veterans that God could make a way for them the same way he was making a way for us. We prayed all the time about the issue and the vets we heard about. There were even some from the rap group that Phil attended. We began to visit many and became acquainted with them and their families. I could see that they were a group of people with genuine leadership skills and giant, giving hearts. The more we heard about the pain they were in, the harder we prayed. The burden wouldn't lift. When I went to pray, in my heart, I would hear a still, small voice saying, "Vets for Christ."

Finally, one day, I asked God to tell me what Vets for Christ was. He told me that it was to be an outreach to Vietnam vets and their families to offer them the hope of God. Many were placing their hope in the government and the government was failing them, leading to despair and demise. The number of veterans of the Vietnam war who committed suicide far exceeded the number that were killed in the war. We knew if they placed their trust in God, he would not fail them. God directed me that VFC was to include a newsletter made up of stories from vets that had come through the tough times, finding God as their source of comfort and healer of their emotional distress.

We began in faith. We were prayerful and took one step at a time. One story we heard involved a vet who tied himself to a tree on the mall in DC and committed suicide. Another, whom Phil knew from his VA rap group would get so far and then off to the woods he would go, leaving his wife and three children for days. No one knew where he went and when or if he was coming back. They moved out of state and kept in touch. They ended up in a church where he became a leader there and they raised their family with positive results. I wrote a tract for the wives of veterans called, "She's Been There." The picture on the front was a silhouette of a woman running away from a helicopter. It was for the women who truly knew they loved their husbands. They didn't know how to get through the pain of PTSD and stay with them. I had already experienced this, so I knew what to say to them. Our slogan was, "From the Boots to the Bible." The scripture that became our guiding verse was clear.

"We comfort others with the same comfort that he has given us."

We were directed to start a mailing list. We found vets that had experienced the saving power of Jesus. Their testimonies filled the first newsletter. Phil wrote a second tract entitled, "The Mission," for those who had already begun their relationship with God and wanted to go on in their walk. Before I went to work at the hospital, I would pray each morning that I would meet another veteran or his family. My prayers were answered, and the list of vets grew rapidly.

The Vietnam Veteran's Wall was finally finished in Washington. Phil was eager to see it. We decided it would also be a good place to reach out to other vets and their families. It also contributed to Phil's healing. We found a competent babysitter for the weekend. We were up at six in the morning to get ready for our trip. Little Tanya was up too. She walked into our bedroom and, bolder than we thought possible for a little girl, made a proclamation.

"Mommy and daddy-The door is open, and the vets are coming out." It was a staggering statement, as if she was proclaiming the future of the outreach. We had gotten button pins in the Vietnam service colors of green and yellow. There was a simple statement on the pin. It read, "Hug a 'Nam Vet Today." We passed them out to the vets at the wall. Everyone loved those pins. There were plenty of tears to go around that cool fall day in DC. Phil found the names of his buddies whom he had lost over there and traced their names, like many did. With each one, he told me the story of what he had experienced. It was a bridge that he had to cross in his journey of healing.

We also learned of veterans in prisons and began sending them the newsletters. Phil had been to Attica during his paralegal work in Rochester, so he knew vets there. We heard of a group of them in Auburn prison. It wasn't long before we went there regularly, bringing our children with us. I was pregnant and we were going into the state prison. I prayed for God to help me write a song that would minister to the hearts of vets. I had never done that before. I wrote "This Lonely Road." My youngest sister helped me arrange it. I read the lyrics to Phil who assured me that it was spot on. I got the song copyrighted. In the prison, Phil preached, and I sang the song. I knew it had reached the hearts when a vet named "Hoss" wrote and requested to have the lyrics sent to him. The power of God was strong as we worked in the prison. Another vet,

Dennis, who had become a Christian prior to our visit, was a regular contact. He loved our family and gave us a framed picture that he dedicated to our children.

As the list grew, we needed more help. We prayed to God to send us a Vietnam vet who was a strong Christian who would help us reach the brothers. I prayed this before work one day. I went to work that morning and was transferred from the medical-surgical unit to the rehabilitation unit. I was a float nurse, so I worked wherever they needed me in the hospital. I was assigned two elderly ladies to care for that day. I went pouting into the solarium.

"Thanks God! I prayed for a Vietnam vet. We need the help! Now, instead, I have two ladies to take care of!"

An hour didn't go by before I was eating my words. Walking down the hall, looking into the rooms, I spotted a patient in a room. He looked like he was Phil's age. My heart skipped a beat. Could it be? I went to the nurse's station and pulled his chart. I saw that he was the same age and had a history of alcohol problems. That was usually a good clue that they might be a vet with PTSD. Many vets ended up with drug or alcohol problems. The divorce rate was sky high. I went back down the hall and walked into the room. I saw tattoos on his folded arms. I took a deep breath and began talking to him.

I introduced myself.

"I saw you in here and I was just wondering if you happen to be a Vietnam veteran?"

"Yes," he said. "Army-Artillery division."

I looked around his room. The curtain was drawn between him and the empty bed beside him. On the curtain, pinned in several places, were papers with scriptures written on them. I couldn't contain the excitement. God was answering again.

"You are a Christian too? We prayed for you this morning!"

He seemed amused at my exhilaration. His wife walked in, and I introduced myself. Then I explained to them about VFC and how it came into existence. It turned out they were people of strong faith. They were down to earth, not some fly-by-nights trying to show off their religious zeal. I looked at his wife. She looked too familiar. I decided to tell her.

"You look like someone we just met."

I told her we had just went to a home bible study in our neighborhood a week prior and that she looked like the woman whose husband taught the bible study.

"That's my sister."

Someone had taught me that there are no coincidences with God. That experience proved again to me that our steps are ordered by God. I knew without a doubt that God was directing us. They became our helpers in the outreach. He and Phil would go out walking in the rough neighborhoods of Syracuse to tell people about the Lord. He would tell them how they couldn't threaten him with heaven. They were a jovial pair, always going out in the joy of the Lord, loving people and praying.

One day, when I was pregnant for Michael, I walked down the street on the West end of the city near where we lived. I so wanted to be a positive influence in the lives of the people there. I walked into a pawn shop and saw a blonde with bright red fingernails and tight jeans who ran the place. I muttered a prayer in my heart.

"God, I want to tell her about you." I began talking. I chickened out when it came to the God part. I left, feeling defeated and foolish. I felt like I had failed God.

A couple of months later, in the summertime, I received a phone call. The call was from the wife of a vet who had heard about Vets for Christ and wondered if we could help. Her husband had been buried alive in Vietnam and survived. He suffered from a major drinking problem. We discovered that we lived close to each other, so I invited her to come to my house. When she got there, she sat at my table telling me about the familiar problems she was going through with her husband. I pulled out my notebook, fully intent to educate her on PTSD. Immediately, I heard a voice within my spirit tell me something different.

"Put away that notebook and just tell her about me."

It was so pronounced that I didn't hesitate to obey. I began to tell her about what we had been through over the last several years and how God had intervened. After a while, she began to cry.

"I'm crying!" she proclaimed.

I thought it was strange that she should make a big deal about something so obvious. I didn't get a chance to speak next.

"You don't understand!" she said. "*He* made me cry. I haven't been able to cry in years!"

She then told me that she had been married once, years before, in Arizona, to another Vietnam veteran. He had mysteriously disappeared and never came back. He was the father of the daughter who lived with her. She explained that she had so much hurt in her life that she had become hardened and unable to cry.

I asked if she wanted to pray with me. She agreed, and there in my kitchen, she became saved. Before she left, she requested that we come to her house on the weekend for a barbecue so Phil could meet her husband, Adrian. We set up the time.

When Saturday came, we traveled ten minutes to their home. While Phil, the kids and Adrian tended the barbecue,

I stood inside talking to my new friend. Suddenly, it was as if blinders fell off my eyes. In front of me was that same woman I had met in the pawn shop! I started to cry at the marvelous faithfulness of God and told her about my trip to her shop and how I had wanted to tell her about God but had chickened out and left, praying for her as I went. Now, in another season, God had sent her to my house and still allowed me to lead her to his throne of grace. Coincidence? There are no coincidences when God is in your life.

VFC continued to grow. We met another vet musician. He learned the song I had written. He accompanied me on his guitar as I sang it. We taped it to share with others. We wrote to a famous country singer to tell him about our outreach. He donated tee shirts and belt buckles with his name on them that we were able to sell in our sale to raise funds for the ministry.

Adrian ended up getting saved and coming to church with his family and us. We became friends. He had a tough go of it. His testimony ended up in the newsletter. He had been buried alive in Vietnam and survived. One night in the early stages of our relationship, he tried to commit suicide by taking rat poison. Phil was able to get him to the hospital. The enemy of our soul is always out to try and destroy anyone who turns their life over to God. Fortunately, he is powerless over God.

Another vet came to live with us since he was getting a divorce and going through trying times. We were in his wedding and used to visit them frequently. He was older and had served in the Army, as well as been a Navy Seal. He turned out to be a family friend.

Time moved on and we were still having financial struggles. Some people wanted to donate to the ministry, so we start a helping hands fund for needy vets. One day we got a letter from a distraught mother of a veteran in Pennsylvania. Her son had suffered three nervous breakdowns since Vietnam. In addition to that, several tornadoes had ransacked the area he lived in, leaving his home destroyed. She asked if we could send any money to help him. Phil went to pray. At the time, we only had thirty dollars in the fund. He came downstairs from prayer.

"God wants us to send sixty dollars," he told me.

"How can we do that? We only have thirty dollars in the account?" I was visibly upset. His answer came clearly and boldly.

"If we obey, God will take care of us. He tells us to live one day at a time."

He wrote out the check for sixty dollars and sent it. Within three days, three times that amount came in as donations. We were learning what it means to step out in faith.

The money that was donated was kept for VFC only. We had a friend who volunteered his work to illustrate for our tracts, newsletters, business cards and anything else we needed We also had a printer who volunteered his printing press services for it all. God was providing every step of the way.

One day we got a notice in the mail that our house was going to be sold. Our gracious contract holder was older, and her children had advised her to sell the house. Because the deed was in our name, we had the choice to relinquish it to her or try to sell it ourselves. We chose the latter. Phil still had $16,000 in back debt from his previous marriage. We were still on welfare. The house ended up being sold to a young couple. Before we moved out, they had to do some painting and fixing up so their FHA mortgage would go through. We didn't know what to do, but knew we had to move. We decided we would try to rent a house instead of an apartment. That became a major focus of our prayer, since our time to be out of that house was coming up quickly.

One day we decided to go for a drive and lean on God for his leading concerning where we would live next. We drove all over. We headed north of the city. We passed a street called Davis Road. Phil felt a very strong sense that we should go down that road, but it had been a long day and we were exhausted, so instead of following the prompting, we went home. We decide to call a rental agency to see if anyone knew of any houses that might be for rent. We couldn't afford more than five hundred dollars a month. An agent called us back on one of the following days.

"There's a house for rent for $500. Apparently, the owner went through a divorce and can't afford to keep it. Go to North Syracuse. Turn left on Davis Road. It's off Caughdenoy Rd. The house is on the corner of Davis and Imperia Lane."

As sheep we never seem to learn. God delivers us time and time again. He parts the Red Seas in our lives and gives us manna perpetually. Yet we forget or doubt. When Phil hung up the phone, we had to repent for not following the directions God had tried to give us only days before. We went to see the three-bedroom spit level home. It had a park and playground behind it and was in a nice development with good schools. Our daughter was about to enter third grade. We signed the contract. Our church helped us move. The ladies even helped me make beds and unpack the boxes in the kitchen. We were good to go.

As we had learned, God always does exceedingly, abundantly above all we could ask or think, he was doing it again. We profited $16.87 from the sale of the house. That was after Phil paid off the $16000 debt and we paid welfare back. We were cleared to start all over.

In the new house, we used the downstairs as a recreation room. There was also room for an office and a laundry room. David, Thomas, and Rabeccah, Phil's three children, would have plenty of room to stay when they visited, and when they did, they ended up going to the church family camp with us. Michael was still in the crib and since the elder two were so young, they shared a room. Toys dominated the basement level. I began to take per diem work at various agencies doing high tech cases which involved patients on respirators. I was paid good for my work and still had flexibility. VFC continued to grow. We literally had hundreds of vets that our mailing covered. We were communicating with vets in prisons and hospitals across the country. We even had a vet in Kenya and some in Canada writing to us.

Before long I started to feel God's prompting again. It was getting stronger. Our pastor and wife were helping us with the mailings. We had to acquire a bulk mail permit. I kept feeling that God was telling us to work full time, in faith, in the outreach. We were already operating in faith for groceries. Phil would go upstairs to pray and I would pray downstairs while watching the children. He would get a number as he prayed.

"The Lord told me sixty dollars."

"That's the same number I got!"

Off I would go to get groceries. Inevitably, within the next couple of days, the amount that we were told in prayer was paid for. Some would call it writing bad checks We called it writing checks in faith as God led us. The day came when I told Phil about the promptings I had been getting.

"I am hearing from God that we are supposed to do this ministry full time, trusting God for the finances, even for our rent."

Phil didn't know what to say but agreed to pray about it. He would get up early and go walking in the park behind our house. By that time, he had gotten a job at a local pancake restaurant where he would walk to. It wasn't long before God confirmed the next step to him. We were in harmony and took the step. Two friends volunteered to help with the ministry, functioning as our secretaries.

Once again God was forever faithful as we worked getting the word to veterans. God proved himself true every step of the way. One day I needed panty hose to wear to an event and had none. I prayed for some. People would think that was lunacy. I knew that God provided everything. That very day, in our mailbox, was a free pair of panty hose that happened to come as a gift from a company. Another time we needed groceries. I was impatient. We only had one-hundred dollars I went to the store and bought groceries without praying first. When I got home that day, a phone call came. Our friend worked at the railroad.

"Fran, a train car came in damaged and it's full. When they asked if I knew anyone who might be able to use some food, I gave them your name. They are on their way to your house. There was pork roast, butter, and all kinds of things. I had to repent again for being anxious and not waiting on the Lord for his direction.

Chapter 8:
Battles and Blessings

Life was never without battles. We knew without a doubt we were in the center of God's will. He proved himself time and time again. Phil had shared what God was doing with us in his combat rap group. It didn't take long for Sterling to show up at our door. He had been a Black Beret in Vietnam. He was sworn to secrecy about some of the missions he had been on. In fact, in one conversation he told us that he had been told that if he divulged any of the things he had taken part in, he would be killed.

The reason Sterling showed up at our door was because he had been stirred by Phil's testimony. Growing up, he had been raised in a Baptist church and at one time had a relationship with God, even participating as youth leader. Now he wanted to learn more. He asked Phil to teach him some bible studies. Sometimes he would come to our house and other days we would go to his, in the woods, in Tully, south of the city. We became acquainted with his wife and children. Our children all got along great. It was there that we shared our recipes for the government food we were all on. Since cheese was one of the items we received, cheese soup became a famous one that all the kids loved. It didn't help anyone's cholesterol, but we were all happy when we were sharing that or the canned pork. The guys thought of it like glorified C-rations.

Phil and Sterling became quite close before his family moved up north near the Black River. We heard that someone from his past was trying to frame him regarding an old drug deal. His marriage was going through a rough time and life was becoming stormy for him. We didn't hear from them again.

I started a support group for the wives of Vietnam vets. I learned that those who knew many of these wives failed to see the problems the vets were going through. They labeled them as crazy. It had helped me to meet other wives of vets as we were suffering alongside our guys with the issues. I knew it would help others. The group was called, "WOVVS." (Wives of Vietnam Veterans) One woman came from Rome, an hour away. She had an eight-month-old baby. She told of how her husband, in Vietnam, was going to pick up a baby to save it but the baby had been boobytrapped and exploded. Because of that, his emotions were scarred. He refused to pick up their baby because it would trigger flashbacks. My husband used to tell me that this was a common thing over there. Many of the Vietnamese believed in reincarnation. They thought the babies would be reincarnated. That helped me to understand why, during the difficult days for him, he had kept repeating, "Life is cheap."

One day a realtor showed up at our door. She had a look of alarm on her face when she questioned the house number as I spoke with her at the door.

"I was told by the owner that this house was empty."

"Do I look like a ghost?" I retorted.

She then went on to tell us that our landlord had put our house on the market. Apparently, when he went through his divorce, he hadn't paid the bank, or the lawyers and his only option was to sell his house. We were faithful renters. He had not said anything about this to us. It wasn't the first time he had lied to us. It was the last straw as far as Phil was concerned. He called him.

"Harry! You have lied to us many times. You won't get away with this. God tells us that he will bless those who have blessed us and curse those who curse us."

Of course, our landlord was caught between a rock and a hard place, didn't like any of this. The house was going on the market, and we had to find another place to live.

Phil was still doing some landscaping. One of the attorneys he worked for was an investor and had a house for rent in Lysander, which was a village north of us. It was vacant and he was willing to rent it to us for six hundred dollars a month. I began packing again. While I was packing some things in the basement, a piece of paper came drifting to the floor. It was the prayer list I had put together when we lived at the previous house. At the time of making the list, I had sat down with my little ones to compose a list of our dream house. I was tired of the transients, the cherry bombs, and tired of the PTSD days. The list included four bedrooms, a wood stove, laundry facilities, a fenced, safe yard and an office for our outreach. Swing set was on the list, too, but I had crossed it off as if it was difficult for God. I grumbled some inaudible thing and stuffed the paper in the box.

A couple of weeks later, we went to see the house in Lysander. I didn't realize it at first, but the house had everything on our prayer list and more. It even had a swing-set and a fort for the kids. The people before had added on a great room with a wrap-around deck. When the breeze blew, the scent of lilacs from the yard drifted into the room. Flowers bloomed all around the stockade fence. Each season produced a new crop of perennials. Phil always made sure I had fresh flowers on the table all the time. The master bedroom had a picture window that overlooked two birch trees that I called the "dancing trees."

There was even a detached garage with a huge office in it. It was in a quiet setting in the country and the yard was large enough for children and a dog. It was lacking a refrigerator. We loved the house but concluded that we couldn't afford the rent plus the money for a new fridge. We went home, loving the house, but discouraged.

"We just have to surrender it to God." I told Phil. "If it is his will, he will make a way for us."

A week later, I remembered that prayer list, realizing that everything on the list was at that house. Phil took the list to the attorney, who was amazed that something written a couple of years ago matched his house perfectly. He and his partner decided to buy the refrigerator for us. He even told Phil that he could work off the rent by doing landscaping for him and some of his friends. God had made a way for us again. We left the house with the backyard park and moved again

It was a pleasure to live there. The neighbors were wonderful. The postmaster and his wife lived across the street. He plowed our driveway in the winter as if it was his own and never charged a penny. Another older couple babysat our children when we went off on a weekly basis to teach a home bible study. Still driving that Vega, we traversed the thirty-five miles to church and back three times per week. By this time, Phil was in charge of maintenance, and I was the piano player. We would get there early for the prayer service and Phil would take our youngest, Michael, into the pre-service prayer with him. Often on the way, the whole family would be singing hymns as we drove the distance. We were happy.

Money was still tight. We operated VFC for a long time before Phil started to get sick. He would go off to do some work and come home early, telling me that he was running out of energy too early and sometimes becoming short of breath. We quickly learned in those days that stress was a common diagnosis for a lot of vets. Eventually, Phil decided that we would no longer continue the outreach. He said he realized that part of the reason he had been doing it was for his own healing. While that was true, I disagreed with his decision. That didn't change anything. Something was changing and life started getting stormy again.

The two oldest children were taking the bus to school. They had a long ride. Michael was just beginning to talk. Kindergarten for Chris was half days, so I had to be there when he got home from school. His favorite after school snack was fresh, raw vegetables. Tanya loved her own room. Since the yard was fenced, and I had a huge corner window, I could let Michael outside to play and watch him from the kitchen. We went on family walks nightly, greeting the neighbors as we went.

With the move and Phil's new health problems, there wasn't much income. I drove thirty-five miles to my evening job a few nights at the University Medical Center. I had to. Our caveman car was not inspected and registered on time.

One night, coming home from the bible study we were teaching, Phil was exceeding the speed limit. A policeman stopped us. Suddenly, they were taking Phil out of the car and putting him in handcuffs. They said his name showed up on their computer and didn't explain to me exactly why they were taking him. One of the policemen followed me home. The other took Phil to the station. Hours later he was brought home by another officer. For some reason they had his name in their computer and there was a mix up. That didn't negate the fact that the insurance and registration still needed dealing with. A week later we got the notice that his license was going to be suspended and that we owed the state hundreds of dollars in fees due to late registration. On top of that, he could possibly face jail time because of it.

Phil had a good friend who was the brother he never had. He and his wife went to church with us. He agreed to go to the court with Phil when he had to face the music for the car problems. It was on the Thursday before Easter. They stood together before the female judge. Phil told her about his recent illness, financial difficulties, and that he was a born-again Christian. The judge was enlightened and said that because it was Holy Thursday, she was dropping all the charges. as She ordered him to get the car business taken care of within the next couple of weeks. Somehow, he was able to get the money together to do that. Case closed. God had made a way again. It could have turned out much worse.

We began listening to a preacher on the radio that our friends told us about. The sermons were about the end times. God began to show us things in the scriptures that were contrary to what we had been taught. We went somewhere in Pennsylvania with our kids to listen to the man preach at someone's home. They let us spend the night. On the way down, our muffler broke. The people we stayed with fixed it for us with no charge. The sermons provoked us to delve deeper into the bible. Phil would spend two hours daily in bible study in the early morning hours. I saw his life change as a result of it. He seemed more sensitive and long-suffering. There was a problem with our new preacher friend though. He always started by talking about what was in the news.

"Don't you Christians read the news? Bunch of dummies."

His words came quickly, harsh and condemning. Truth was mingled with criticism. I tried to ignore the criticism and just choose the truth. We drove home, on fire for the new thing we were learning, and overlooked his attitude.

We found out that this preacher had a Christian community in South Carolina. That led to us to meet a couple that was about to move there. We visited their home. They lived in a house on a wooded lot east of Syracuse. They home schooled their children. It wasn't long after meeting them that we decided we would move to the town outside of the community. We planned to get jobs and check out the place. If we liked what we saw, perhaps one day we would move there.

Phil decided we needed to sell things to make our trip lighter. He believed we were doing the right thing. It was 1987. We sold all kinds of stuff that had sentimental value. That included the pine poster bed that my father had given me. That went quickly, followed by the wicker rocker that had been my grandmother's when my mom was a baby. He also sold his medals from the war and the honeymoon wheel we had created from decoupaged pictures of our trip to New Orleans. Phil was outside making the sales and I was inside crying my heart out.

"He just doesn't have the love! Something is wrong!" I proclaimed.

It didn't make a difference. I was trying to be a submissive wife. Every day I would pray, hundreds of times.

"God don't let us be misled. Please don't let us go to the left or the right."

My parents were furious. If they could have, they would have had the FBI trail us. They feared that we were going to some type of cult. They came over and took pictures of our kids and brought them gifts thinking they might never be able to see us again. We continued, until the house, along with the piano and the china closet, was rented out to someone else. We literally had scaled down to a trailer load of belongings by the time we left.

I had already quit my job at the University hospital. Phil had a week left as a telephone operator at the VA hospital. He decided we would move to an efficiency apartment in Fayetteville to wait out the week. In the meantime, the preacher down south knew we were selling and coming down. I was still crying and worried. I was saddened by all the things we didn't have anymore, but somehow deluded into thinking we were doing the right thing. It felt free not to be bound by the material possessions we once had. At the one room efficiency, Phil went to work, and I took the kids for walks. I was still asking God not to let us go the wrong way.

The night before we were supposed to leave, Phil called the preacher and told him we were all set to leave in the morning. He was confronted with wrath. It was strange, because the other family had already told him we were coming.

"You're coming down here? God hasn't told me that you are supposed to come here!"

I don't remember what Phil said to him but by the end of the conversation, the door was slammed shut in our faces. We were not going there. Our stuff was gone, my job was gone, our dream home was gone, and we had no idea where on earth we were going with only Phil's income. Deep down, I breathed a sigh of relief, knowing that God had his hand on us. He was protecting us from what later turned out to be a false prophet. To this day I am thankful that my children did not end up on this commune-like community, picking okra. We would all have been subject to the control of this critical man who told us the world was ending. The last time I checked, he was headed to jail.

That night, we went over to my parent's house. They weren't home, but they had given us the key to their house. We went in to wait until they came home. I don't think I've ever seen them as happy as they were when we told them our plans had fallen through. The family was restored.

Chapter 9:
The Little Apartment

We needed to find a place to live in a short amount of time. We ended up finding an apartment in a town called Warners, only three miles away from my parents. The upstairs apartment was in an old Victorian house. It was very little, unlike the former houses we had lived in. A grand, polished oak staircase led up to the apartment. There was a minimum of kitchen cupboards, three small bedrooms, a living room and a room at the far end of the house we made into the dining room. It had a big backyard with blueberry bushes. The girls downstairs were married which was a strange thing in those days. They were friendly and greeted us with some of their baked goods. The house was near a very dangerous corner and the train tracks were close enough to hear the passing trains. The house rattled many times a day. When we moved. we had no beds for the kids. We had a convertible couch that weighed a ton, and not much more, since we had sold so much.

One weekend we had forty dollars to find beds for the kids at garage sales. Phil became quickly discouraged and didn't want to look anymore. I was fighting it too, questioning God about how on earth we would find the things we needed for a mere forty dollars. We drove home. Something welled up inside of me and I told Phil that I was going to take the money and go find beds for our children. I dropped them off at the apartment and drove out of town on the big hill, determined to win.

"God, you told us we have not because we ask not! I am asking you to somehow take these forty dollars and help me find beds for our children!"

The first sale I stopped at was ten minutes away. An elderly couple was selling their belongings so they could move to a smaller place. There I found a full-size bed for fifteen dollars. That would be for our daughter. I drove to the next town and found another garage sale. There was a maple twin bed for ten dollars in perfect condition. This could be for our son, Chris. I decided to stop and visit my cousin. I told him what was going on. He told me his son had just gotten a waterbed and I was welcome to have the twin bed he wouldn't be using anymore. The bed they gave me was an identical match to the twin bed I had just purchased! God was good and I was elated. Now there was a bed for Michael too. I still had money left and I had the three beds we needed! I drove to another sale and got a couple of lamps. I ended up going home that day with more than beds. God indeed had done exceedingly abundantly above all I could ask or think. Phil was baffled and overjoyed at the same time as we set up the beds for the night.

The little apartment was home, but its tiny size was getting on my nerves. One morning I couldn't find our little son. When I did, he had snuck all the way down the stairs and outside. He had my white nursing shoes on. He was wearing his brother's jacket. When I found him, he was already off the porch. I was upset thinking that he could have wandered into the road at any time at that dangerous corner. I caught him just before he made it.

The other children would take the bus to school every day. They were in first and third grade. Kids on the bus bullied my son, making fun of his hat. We had to deal with that issue. The other issue was the girls downstairs. This was in the eighties and things were different in society than they are today. It was time to go. We had been there a year.

One good memory that came out of it was my daily walks to the post office with my youngest son. Every day we walked down the street to get the mail while the others were in school. We played a little game by the big oak doors of the house when we got back. I would go in and close the door most of the way. He would stand outside and knock. I then opened the door, pretending I was a surprise visitor.

"Hello. Who's there? Michael?" I would say with a lilted voice.

He would get all excited and start smiling and laughing. It became a routine that's one of those things a mother always remembers. Our family walks to pick blueberries behind the Catholic church is another of the fond memories.

While we were there, we had no church to go to, having been extricated from the one we'd been attending for sharing things we had learned from the scriptures. They canceled a church get together one night with other churches to have a meeting about the subject. They taped the meeting, and we were given a copy. At the meeting, the pastor told the people that we had gone off believing in something different than them, even though that organization held the same beliefs, depending upon which church you attended. He made a comment.

"Maybe one day our brother and sister will come home."

In the meantime, God was dealing with us about the fact that we had become pharisaical. We thought we had all the answers and looked down at others thinking they didn't have all the wisdom, revelation, and knowledge that we had been given. We began to learn about God's love for everyone, not just a select group. One day after quite some time praying, Phil made an announcement.

"We are free to love anyone with God's love. We can go back and visit that church."

We went back to visit. The service went on. During the greeting time, the pastor taped Phil on the shoulder.

"Brother Phil, it would have been better if you had come with an invitation."

We left, suddenly what we had learned about the love that didn't really exist in a church that seemed more like an elite club. Instead, it seemed to exist only for the members.

Chapter 10:
Evicted By Ants

It was time to move on. I prayed that we could find a house with privacy instead of an apartment to rent so the children would have a yard and freedom. Our credit was still not good enough to buy house. I found a job at another hospital, working per diem and evenings on an obstetrics and gynecology floor. We found a house for rent in a near town. It was a four-bedroom home in a nice suburb on a quiet street. It had a swing set in the back yard. The rent was seven hundred a month, but we felt we could afford it.

Soon we moved in. Family walks around the block were again part of our lives, with Michael driving his big wheel and the other children on their bikes. By this time, Phil had gotten a job working eleven hours daily as a banquet steward for the Sheraton Inn. It was hours before the kids got to see their dad. Whenever there was a late wedding or banquet, he would bring home an extra plate of food. Sometimes it was prime rib.

I met a patient who lived a block over from us. Her name was Mary Jane. She had multiple sclerosis. Her husband was gone a lot. He remodeled their home so that it was functional for her disability. It had stove and cupboards at wheelchair height. She needed someone to come and help her go through some of her closets, so I offered to help. Little did I know that someday my situation would be similar. I took my daughter with me once. It was a good feeling to know that we were helping someone.

Phil had to go to court in Colorado for hearings about the custody of his other three children. He was gone for two weeks. I missed him like crazy, but I knew he was getting some long-lost time with his three children whom he missed dearly. In the meantime, I continued to work at the hospital on the evening shift. At night, I would arrive home from my job around 11:30. My knees creaked as I walked up the stairs to observe my sleeping angels from retiring.

We began to see carpenter ants creeping around. They marched down the dining room walls when we had company for dinner. I saw some in my daughter's bedroom. There were too many to go unnoticed. We needed to get them exterminated, but we needed permission from the landlord. For some reason, he was adamant about it and refused to permit an exterminator to take care of the problem. Phil called our energy provider. They came to inspect the walls. The man told us that though this was a nice-looking house, cosmetically, in a nice neighborhood, that there was moisture in the walls, causing them to have the type of dry rot that is found in houses in the inner city. He further explained that the way it had been built, moisture collected in the walls, hence, the ants.

Even though we took good care of the property and paid our rent on time, the landlord sent us a letter of eviction. We couldn't afford a lawyer. I began to do research which led me to discover that the ant problem was breaching our warranty of habitability. We began to get our case together. We should represent ourselves. The lady next door wrote a letter attesting to the neglect of the landlord in issues she had with him. Phil stuffed a baggie in a crack on the back wall of the house. The next day, the baggie was full of water. We had a bucket of rotten siding, along with pictures and letters. We went to court and the judge wasn't even going to hear our case.

"I'm sure Mr. X wouldn't have purchased a $90,000 house knowing there was a problem with the construction."

He finally listened to us, looked at our evidence, and then he, the landlord, and the lawyer, all went into another room. Now I knew what a kangaroo court was. They returned a short while later, stating that we were going to evicted. We couldn't believe it. We were told we had thirty days to move.

Chapter 11:
The Stucco Villa

"Where are we going mom?"

I was washing the dishes when one of the kids asked me the question. I kept washing the dishes, feeling distraught, and tried to muster all the confidence I could.

"I don't know, but God does." I retorted, trying to keep from crying. The truth was that I had no idea where we would go. We were not able to buy a house at that time. We had both changed jobs. Phil was no longer working at the restaurant job. I had gotten a job as a shift director at the Rescue Mission, working in the Alcohol Crisis Center on the evening shift. This opened the door for Phil to work there. He got the position of Food service manager.

He was finally back on days and though challenged, he loved his job. He had full accountability for the way the food service was done for the homeless, and the men and women in the rehabilitation programs. He was also in charge of food service for the elderly men in the adult home. He was told he saved the mission thirty-thousand dollars his first year there. Despite that, he improved it. He went to the farmer's market on his own time on Saturday mornings and purchased items for the salad bar he set up in the cafeteria. He conferred with a dietician and set up specialty meals for the different cultural groups represented. There were raving reports from the people he served, and he was well loved by his employees. He took our children there to volunteer often. If they weren't helping in the office with clerical duties, they were assisting as prep cooks in the kitchen, or helping in the office. We would take the children to visit the men in the adult home. We invited one of them to our house for Thanksgiving.

To us it was all about the love. We weren't the conventional couple. When we were told to limit our relationships to the workplace only, we rebelled. In fact, one young man caught our hearts. He was in his early twenties, intelligent and handsome. He had gotten caught up in drugs and ended up living at the Mission in the rehab program. And day he walked in with a briefcase and told the staff he had a bomb. These were the days before terrorism as we see it today. They went ballistic. He didn't really have a bomb but that's what he told them. This was in the nineties. Somehow, he was allowed to stay in the program. He had already been in and out of it several times. Our whole family loved him. We ended taking him over to our house for dinner and became friends with him. To us, that was the gospel in action. Enough was already being done to preach to people from a distance. They needed to see the love of God manifested from the people who claimed to have it. We never had any problems with him.

Phil made a staff friend at the Mission. He and his wife had two children that were the same ages as ours. We often shared dinners together and sometimes babysat each other's kids so the parents could get a break. He and his wife offered to store our stuff in their garage. That was a load off our minds, since we weren't sure where we would end up. We had to find a place to rent, and hopefully it would be a house. I always pushed to rent a house with a yard for the kids, and later, one that allowed us to have pets. We scoured the papers.

We found a place for rent in North Syracuse, about fifteen minutes from where we were. We went to look at the beige, stucco house with an attached garage. It was a ranch, near the corner of two main residential streets in the neighborhood. It had three bedrooms with a master bedroom that was added onto the back of the house. The yard was huge. On one side was another house, and on the other side was a wooded lot. Two landlords shared the ownership. It was vacant and ready. We decided we would take it. The place reminded me of a little villa in the summertime. The kids loved the big yard.

Winter was another story in that master bedroom. It was so cold in there that I was able to keep pies refrigerated on a table there for Thanksgiving. Ice formed on the inside of the windows in the bathroom. There was a window overlooking the backyard. We would often find deer romping in the early morning hours. The other end of the house, where the children slept, was warm. It was a lovely place to live, except for the freezing part.

We decided to have a big garden. That, of course, had to be done with Phil's composting. After we unpacked the boxes, he flattened them and laid them out with newspaper in a large area of the yard. It irritated me to see that stuff back there. He then added his compost mixture of onion and potato skins, and anything else we threw away, to the soil. I remember joking with him that made if he added eggshells, we could grow eggs. That only served to put the idea in his head that we should get chickens. That didn't fly, but the garden grew greatly.

Our son, Chris, decided to don his raccoon hat and venture into the wilderness in the field next door. He put his hat on and went there daily to do his exploring. He loved it. I remember him telling me about it.

"Mom, I'm going to live in the wild when I get older."

"Oh, you'll be interested in girls and want to get married someday." I retorted.

He denied that vehemently by the next comment.

"Yuk!" He responded.

We hired a guitar teacher who played in a local band to come to the house and give Chris lessons. He liked that as well. Today he is married with a little boy who is a marvel!

Our daughter, Tanya, loved her own room at that place. She was busy with her violin lessons. Her teacher also came to our house. We had already begun home schooling the two older children. Michael was the youngest and he went to half-day kindergarten. He was a kinetic learner, and he became bored with things easily. He didn't even like to sit down and color. His biggest aspiration at the time was his desire to go back to school for the first grade. He finally told me the reason.

"I want to go back there so I can eat in the cafeteria." He never did. We ended up having to move again later.

Our home was rich with music. Besides the guitar and the violin, Mike pounded the bongos. It was ironic because a few years later he ended up being a drummer.

"He's a natural." The teacher told this after his first lesson.

My niece would come over with her violin and they all put on a little concert for us. They were fun times.

There was a stray cat that kept coming and meowing incessantly in our windows. Phil checked with the neighbors. No one owned the cat. It was a mottled gray color. In the early summer mornings, Michael would be up early and in the backyard. I looked out one morning and saw him playing with that cat. Then I saw Phil sneak in a box of food he had gotten at the store across the street. That was when I gave in.

"Ok. You don't have to hide it anymore. I'll pay for the shots."

Erica was the chosen name for the cat that came to stay with us for many years. Of course, before we could get her spayed, she got pregnant. I remember being up in the middle of the night playing midwife while she had her kittens on the garage steps. Of course, we couldn't keep those kittens. We took a box to the farmer's market with us and made a sign. "Free kittens." Thankfully, they all found homes that day.

I began working for an agency a couple of days per week so I could homeschool the kids and help with the finances. I did high tech private duty cases. I had patients with ALS and other sicknesses. Many were on respirators and required a nurse who could manage their regimens. Phil was still working at the Rescue Mission. He walked the long distance to take the bus to work each day so I could have the car to use at home.

There was a huge weeping willow tree in front of the house. It was beautiful until the day Phil found the roots coming up into the sump pump in the basement. There was not anything we could do about it, since we were renters. Too soon, the landlords decided they wanted to sell the house. Once again, we were subject to landlords and had to find another place to live. We found a four-bedroom colonial to rent back in the city of Syracuse. By that time, it cost $725 a month to rent a house. It was a lovely older home with a porch and a double city lot. It had a fireplace and gleaming hardwood floors. There was also a detached garage. It was on the East side the city. The further up the hill you went, the richer the people got. The further down the hill you went, the poorer the people were.

It was June when we had to move, and it was very hot. We were sweating, packing and cleaning. I was scrubbing the walls, which had become spotted with fingerprints. In one place I scrubbed so hard that it revealed some orange paint below. Phil was sweeping the basement clean. One of the landlords came in and saw us working. He took a finger to the top of a heat register and stuck it in my face, showing me the dust, insinuating we weren't cleaning enough. I lost it.

"You see we are cleaning this place! That's ridiculous! You are just hoping you can rent this out as soon as we leave without doing what is your lawful duty of painting! I have pictures of what we have been doing. Furthermore, I hope you have a heart attack!" He mumbled something about having pictures too and walked out.

That was far from the love of God that was supposed to be exemplified in my life, but I was fed up with the nonsense we had been subjected to by landlords. We had paid our rent on time and kept places clean, unlike some who didn't and trashed places before disappearing. He just got the brunt of my frustration. At that point, we couldn't wait to get out of there. We looked like hillbillies when we finally loaded up. The top of the car had plants and a pet cage, and who-knows-what-else up there. Finally, we were one our way down the highway with the last load. After a long day in the heat, our nerves were frayed. The children were our busy little helpers. It started to thunder. Phil was throwing stuff off the truck, including a small typewriter I had managed to get him from a food pantry the previous Christmas.

"Why do we need all this stuff? God, just strike me dead!"

After the long, harrowing time of moving again, we settled into the house. It had a finished attic with a skylight that we made into our school room. We loved it. That was the second time since we were married that Phil and I lived on that street. The first was when we moved from Rochester before the kids were born. At that time, we lived in an apartment at the bottom of the hill.

The week we moved; the church was preparing to have an evangelist come to speak. He was from South Africa. I informed my husband that I had enough.

"I'm tired of these men in three-piece suits coming from all over to be guest preachers! I will go see him once and if he is not from God, I am NOT going back!"

We attended the first night. He spoke in his British accent as he told his testimony. He said God had directed him and his family to come to America to restore the joy that the American Christians had lost. He certainly was anointed by God. The joy of God filled the place and touched our family. Laughter spread like wildfire in the meetings. It reminded me of the night we were filled with the Holy Ghost. The joy and love were so thick they were palpable. Even the children were touched by this powerful event. Many of us, including my son, Chris, were struck by the power of God and found ourselves "stuck" to the floor until the Spirit was done with us. A local reporter attended a meeting and Chris got his picture in the paper. One night after the meeting, a group of people in several cars went to the local grocery store after church. This was a common thing after church. Many times, we'd all go to a restaurant together. Tanya got out of the car, staggering like she was drunk and laughing. It was right out of the book of Acts where they accused the men of being drunk at only nine in the morning. One of the people from another car walked over to us. Tanya touched his head, and he was out. He was prostate on the parking lot laughing out loud. There was no denying the presence of God who was doing a mighty work in his people. It was beyond our understanding.

We ended up going for several nights until the meetings were finished. On several of the nights, Phil would get several of the guys from the Rescue Mission to go with us. I had a friend who was like a second mother to me. She was my mom's friend and had babysat us when we were kids. She had been diagnosed with stomach cancer. It was severe enough that she had to go to Roswell Park in Buffalo for her treatments. That was where the most difficult cases were sent. After talking with her, she decided to join us one night. It was there that she was healed of the cancer. She never had to return to Roswell Park or receive treatments again. She lived a good long life. In fact, I got to see her years later. I dreamt that she was in a nursing home. I called the nursing homes around me and found that sure enough, she was there and had just been admitted the day before. I visited her and then she passed away a few days later.

God is good and He was showing us his love in a new way. I was blessed that my whole family was experiencing this. Experiences with God are something that no man can take away. It puts a smile on my face today, in this world of skepticism, to know what we experienced was real.

As difficult as that move was and all that it entailed, life began to get better. Phil had his job at the Mission and was well established by that time. I finally got into a steadier per diem job as a public health nurse in an agency where I used to work as a home health aide when I was in college. One day I realized that we had become more independent, but our faith didn't seem as strong. We didn't seem to need God as much when we both had good jobs and things were going smoother. I remember clearly realizing that fact. It wasn't long after that when life changed abruptly, and we would need faith to survive the days ahead.

Chapter 12:
The Attic School Room and Beyond

Phil was a teacher at heart. Despite everything, when he was able, he was always doing new things with our children. He eagerly assembled an abacus for our daughter. She hated math in public school at the third-grade level and he was determined to change that. With great diligence, he completed the project for his princess.

He also hired an artist and impersonator named Art to teach all three children lessons with pastels. On the days that I worked, I would come home and hear Ronald Reagan, Elvis, or some other celebrity teaching the class upstairs. Parrots and butterflies were drawn, modeled after pictures the kids found in "National Geographic" magazine. These were displayed on the huge wooden easel that he constructed.

Lessons with dad were never boring. I can still see the eyes of the children, then ages thirteen, eleven and eight as he presented his carefully researched lesson on "El Nino." He taught them about how the great flood changed the shape and place of the continents. Many afternoons were spent outside in the driveway teaching them street games he learned growing up in Brooklyn. Sometimes, the four of them would go to the bowling alley or the park down the hill to learn tennis. All five of us would go on bikes to the duck pond where an interesting hike awaited us through the fields and the reed grass. He had a seat on the back of his bike where our youngest child, Michael, would ride on these outings. The thing I didn't see were times he got upset. The kids told me that once he kicked in the small electric heater and smashed the globe because he was impatient about something. I learned more about this later in life when it was too late to change it. I think he was getting increasingly impatient with his lack of ability to carry things out like he used to.

He always stirred everyone's curiosity on our trips to Lake Ontario. Walks along the rocky shore for hours led us to carry loaded pails of interesting rock specimens home. At one campsite near the sandy shore, we found humongous sand dunes to climb and slide down. In winter, snow brought sledding trips that involved some risk-taking. Standing on one ski and sliding down the hill was a challenge. One time while he was at work, the children and I went to the nature center for a snowshoeing adventure. The occasional tapping of a woodpecker kept us company as we tried to keep our balance going over the snowy trail. It was a precious memory I treasure when I think of my early mothering days.

We had a good schedule. He worked four ten-hour days with Wednesday off. I went to work on that day. The mid-week change was good for everyone. On some of his workdays at the Rescue Mission, he took the children with him. They learned meal planning and stockroom organizing. He even brought home inventory sheets and used them for math projects. They learned how to work with food invoices.

The Rescue Mission motto was "Love in Action." One Christmas Eve we bundled up and went to sing Christmas carols at the homes of some of my patients. As a public health nurse, I met many lonely people who had no company for the holidays. The people cried when our little family visited and sang to them. We visited a blind lady and an older vet Phil had met at the Mission. He had a voice box to speak through. The woman sent a thank-you card to the children expressing how much the visit had warmed her heart. She also sent them a dollar each as a little show of her appreciation.

Another time, Phil arranged with a local florist for us to get a deal on some inexpensive plants. On Easter morning, we took the plants and went to visit people in nursing homes who had no families to visit them that day. They cried too. It was a joy to give to others and to teach it to our children.

Then there was Sophie. She was an elderly woman who could hardly move her hands or walk. She barely got around her apartment in the high rise with her walker. She was a patient of mine. Discouragement had gotten the best of her. She told me that she belonged to a church that had a great philanthropic group, yet they never called to help her. There were grocery items she needed.

"I need some things, but no one ever calls to help," she sadly told me.

I made an on-the-spot decision.

"My children and I will come on Wednesday and go get your groceries."

To my amazement, when we got there, she had managed, with great difficulty, to cut out some coupons and make a list for us. We did the shopping and delivered the groceries. She was thankful and overjoyed.

"God must have sent you!" she praised us as if we were angels. It was always a privilege to serve.

Many naysayers tried to tell us that children who were home schooled lacked socialization. I had to correct them by informing them that studies were done that revealed that home schoolers had better socialization skills, since they were not only socialized with the limited group of their peers, but with people of all ages and backgrounds. There were people of all kinds of ethnic and racial backgrounds where we lived. Children who were home schooled interacted with homeless, elderly, and wealthy people as well as peers who fell into a diverse group and other home-schooled children. Our children were rich in social skills. This followed them into their adult years. Their character grew with this enrichment and wasn't stifled by peer pressure that was the main issue with others in the public realm.

In the summer, when they had leftover donations of lettuce and bread at the mission, Phil would bring it home and he and the children would go up and down our street with a wheelbarrow full of food, passing it out to the neighbors. He taught us how to do yard work as he had done when he had his landscaping business. We visited one of my patients and our crew of five worked together outside to revolutionize the elderly woman's yard. She had been unable to go out and pick her own flowers for a long time. Much to her delight, the service was culminated when our daughter picked one of the purple irises and brought it inside to her.

In my nursing rounds, I ran into my tenth-grade English teacher. She was a patient of mine who had a brain tumor. She still managed to work at this stage, writing an article weekly in the local paper called "Good Neighbors." I told her that my husband and I had begun something called, "My Father's Business" to try to meet needs of people in the community. She did an article about us in the paper. We went to a major high-rise for the elderly in the city and introduced our outreach. They welcomed us and the phone was ringing off the hook. The needs were overwhelming. We did what we could.

We met a man in that building who was the sole caregiver for his ninety-two-year-old dad. The man was in his sixties and had not been able to go far for years since he cared for his dad in the wheelchair. He said he would like to go to his class reunion. Phil said he and our boys would provide respite for the man so he could go. They had a blast. The elderly gentleman still had his wits about him. While they were there, they learned that he had been a Syracuse University football player many years prior. He showed them pictures of himself and the team back in the day.

While the guys were taking care of that, my daughter and I went to the South side of town to visit a woman who had, at one time worked at the Rescue Mission. She had recent surgery and was now homebound. We had a nice visit with her as she told us about her family Christmas traditions and many other memories. She verbalized how blessed she was by our visit.

The phone began ringing off the hook. There were more needs than our little family alone could meet. We were in the process of changing our work schedules again so we could devote more time to this endeavor. In the meantime, Dad was always full of surprises.

"What's he bringing home today?"

"Where is he taking us this time?"

"What new thing is he going to teach us today?"

On another visit to Lake Ontario, he taught the children to make a raft out of pieces of driftwood. Then they got to launch their trusty craft onto the waters of the great lake. While I stood on the shore, holding my breath for everyone's safety, I heard their laughter above the sounds of the waves. The lessons he was giving our children in life could never be replaced. Once he told me that God's love is like those waves, it just keeps coming. I have been comforted many times by that little nugget. The value of the things he taught them and the experiences they shared would forever take shape in their characters as they grew.

One day a huge truck pulled up in front of our house. Some men unloaded an upright piano. I had been upset when we almost moved down south because I had to leave the piano. Now someone had donated one to the Rescue Mission. He had gotten it to surprise me. It still stands in my living room today.

Another day a knock at the door produced four women. It was a female barbershop quartet. It was also Valentine's Day. They came into my kitchen and serenaded me with several love songs. I was flabbergasted and blushing. Once again, he surprised me with a gift I never expected and will never forget.

Chapter 13:
Life Changes

The day came when everything changed forever. We had been married for fourteen years. The intrusive ringing of the phone interrupted the hectic routine of the afternoon. I stepped over the pile of laundry and rushed toward the phone. I knew it would be Phil calling as he usually did in the late afternoon for a stress break. It was the same for me because I knew it meant only a short while before he walked through the door, and we could be together again. His voice sounded strained. I felt a momentary flash of nausea. With all the stress he had been under, I wasn't sure what I was going to hear.

"I'm ok. I'm at University Hospital emergency room. Nothing broken. I have some bruises and a laceration on my leg. I was emptying a truckload of food onto a hand truck. I lost my balance and luckily my co-worker caught my head before it hit the cement."

I felt there was more than what he was telling me. Tightness climbed from my toes to my neck as I anticipated what the "something else" might be.

"Four-hundred fifty pounds fell on my right side and knocked me to the ground. They took x-rays of my right leg. I'm waiting for the results."

Four hundred fifty pounds! My mind was already in the car on the way to the hospital. The kids played on the porch in their usual happy manner.

"I'll be home shortly."

"Are you sure you're all right?" I pried with my question, fearing that he wasn't telling me the whole story. He temporarily reassured me that all was under control, and he'd be home soon. I hung up and counted the minutes until he would come through the back door.

Prior to that, in one of our arguments, that I told him he shouldn't become the "Rescue Mission Martyr." He was under an unbearable amount of stress on the job. They never found someone that could walk in his shoes if the job got to be too much. He was manager, buyer and cook. He made deals at the market so the homeless people would eventually enjoy the salad bar he set up for them. He bought various ethnic foods and consulted a nutritionist so he could prepare something tasty for the long lines of homeless people. The first year he was commended for the job he did. He managed, plus he covered for his cooks when they were out. My words of caution went unheeded. He was a driven person and wouldn't listen.

I tried to deny the uneasy feeling in the pit of my stomach. My heart felt like there was a ball and chain around it as it sunk within me. It was April 7, 1992. I was thirty-eight years old, and he was forty-three. My emotions were all over the place. When he came through the door, I examined his bruised leg. He was tired. The emergency room discharge had instructions to report back if he had further problems. He was back in his office the next morning. This time he was limping.

By Christmas, he had to take a leave of absence. He seemed more forgetful and easily agitated. Terrible headaches became the routine and lightheadedness was a daily occurrence. His body began to have intermittent numbness from the waist down. One day, driving home from work before the leave of absence, he drove through a red light without noticing. Much to his chagrin, the car was impounded. The policeman discovered that his license hadn't been renewed on time. Phil limped home and I had to get a neighbor to drive me to get the car out of hock. It cost sixty dollars. It was the extra sixty that we had managed to squirrel away to go for kid's Christmas presents. I needed the car to get to work the next day. Everything was changing too fast.

On his teaching days, he would complete classes for the kids in the morning and fall asleep later on the mattress we put up in the schoolroom. The kids worked independently while he took his nap. He told me the fatigue was so bad it felt like someone had stuck a vacuum cleaner inside of him and sucked all the energy out. That was the first time I really began to understand the exhaustion he was going through. I couldn't imagine having that degree of fatigue continuously.

He started to lose his balance and had coordination problems trying to play basketball with the kids. It also began to affect his driving. Once we almost had an accident when he put his foot on the gas instead of the brake in heavy traffic. His feet were beginning to feel numb, and he couldn't tell which pedal he was pushing. He had to go to the VA for a cane. They discharged him after two weeks of testing.

"It's all subjective-stress." Their broken record got nauseating. In the meantime, Phil's health was digressing.

Chapter 14:
Into the Summer

The sun of late spring was already too hot. The heat made Phil's symptoms worse. The only way to survive was to enjoy the merciful, strong breezes. Unfortunately, the rest of life was not so easy. It was going to be the summer when tangible things became invisible and slipped through our fingers. They were things like homes, promises that would never be fulfilled, and anything else we had planned for a future. It was to be the summer when everything meshed like a rolling snowball escalating with determination to destroy us, if not for God. Life was now a complex stew of marriage struggles, sickness, loneliness, desertion, betrayal, lost relationships, and insecurity.

It began with the great idea that we could, at long last, find a home in the country, buy it, and say goodbye to the land of crass, greedy landlords. We could no longer afford our monthly rent of $725. Besides, the landlord wanted to raise it to $800. Interest rates were low. Opportunity seemed to knock with the advent of a compensation check for Phil, and we began to investigate.

We attempted to dream that we, too, could achieve some American stability at less monthly expense and no corrupt landlord dominance. I set out, for hours at a time, in pursuit of that dream. I became a medieval mistress taking flight. Tasting the possibility of long-awaited freedom from the lorded castles, I pushed forward in search of our home. My searches were diligent, sometimes in fastings, always with prayers, sometimes with singing, always with expectations. Often, I returned to my city dwelling with hope that the next time I would find what had escaped me that day.

The day arrived when I found the house with the hidden pond. It was nestled amongst the trees and wildflowers and was kept by a praying man. It was in a town near our church. Its charm wooed me as I visualized children running in the field and Phil being able to fish. Would God make this way for us if we prayed together with the owner? It seemed as if it had to be God's will. The owner said there was already an offer on the house, but he wanted us to have it and told us he'd be praying that the other deal fell through. For weeks we sat on the edge of our seats, stressed from the waiting that always seems longer when we're anxious. The man was very encouraging. We visited and shared music together. The day came when the door closed. Someone else would do the fishing and running.

My attention again focused on our captivity and my searching grew more intent to find my family our country home. In desperation one night, Phil and I prayed for direction to come soon. The very next day, an investor owner of a four-bedroom ranch on an acre answered positively to the terms we'd prayed about the night before. Taking our $3000, he promised that we could move in on June 16. I didn't mind sitting between all the packed boxes that day. He told me that I would even be able to pick out the colors of our new kitchen and living room carpet. I was delighted.

It would be a home that was big enough for Phil's three other children to come and live with us. My eleven-year-old, Chris, was enthusiastic about the dog he would buy, and I agreed to keep the newborn kittens until we moved there. It even had a wood stove. On subsequent visits we brought two carloads of our strawberries and other plants that Phil had tended with much diligence. On his knees, even though the fatigue caused him to succumb to much sleep, he planted them in the yard that was soon to be ours. He was full of hope, planning how he would landscape the new place, even though he had limitations.

More waiting followed. Many trips to and from the financial empire on the fifth floor of a building in the city kept us busy as we waited for the final approval. The waiting taxed my limits on patience. I was crushed at the end of each day that we'd have to wait until the next day all over again. Days wore into weeks of anticipation. The man with the yellow house grew slack and reneged on his promise for us to take occupancy on June 16. We packed more boxes. One night Phil had a dream.

"Tell Fran 'No' to the yellow house."

I didn't want to hear that because my heart was already set on what I thought was right for us. During our trips out there, we began to get acquainted with the neighbors. Soon we heard that through the years there had been major problems with the water at the place. We talked our landlord into using our security deposit for one more month's rent. Finally, he grew impatient and told us that if we weren't out by July 17, we'd have to pay another month's rent. Because the investor had the only big check we'd had in a long time, we didn't have another month's rent. It tore me apart as he paraded the next renter candidate through our rented palace, showing him the spacious rooms as we sat on boxes and wondered where we'd end up.

We finally did decline the yellow house after people were repeatedly and mysteriously coming up to us and telling us about the problems with the house. God was protecting us. The nice investor kept our $3000. We had to fight and practically threaten him and finally got it back. Then we found another yellow house for sale back in the village. This one had a pool. Once again, the kids were excited. I began to think we were yo-yos. The insurance company ineptly messed up Phil's compensation. By July 12, we still had no mortgage financing. Our income wasn't fixed now due to the insurance company's errors, and it wasn't enough for the bank to grant us the money. We had only days to get out of our house in the city. Where would we go?

By this time, the doctors were hinting around about a serious neurological problem with Phil. The first one we went to diagnosed it as "possible demyelinating disease." I ran home and dug up my Merck Manual. There I read the full gamut of demyelinating diseases and allowed myself to be filled with more fear. Then came the day when another neurologist gathered the symptom history from Phil and automatically deducted that he was sure what it was. We went through seventeen doctors, and it still wasn't definite. This doctor said he thought it was multiple sclerosis. I was relieved that there was no brain tumor, but MS has no cure either. I tried to pray reality away.

The VA sent my weary husband to the Albany hospital, three hours away, to have an MRI done. That ended up in a war between the VA doctors and me. Why did my husband, who was now having leg pain in addition to a myriad of other symptoms, have to travel three hours away in a van, in pain, when there were at least six MRI machines in Syracuse? I was told, in essence, that it had to do with the economy of the VA. It was less expensive for them to send the vets to Albany than to send them to one of the local places. To make it worse, the doctor's orders were once again screwed up and Phil had to end up going twice to complete what should have been done on the first trip. I took him the second time. The children and I didn't know that would be the first in a long series of trips with daddy to clinics and long hours spent in waiting rooms. We would bring their books. They completed their assignments as we waited. We couldn't afford a sitter. I needed to be with Phil because his memory was already becoming affected.

His balance worsened. A two-week hospitalization at the VA produced no change. That experience alone was enough to add to the stress. The inept, negligent things that occurred during those weeks had my stomach in knots. There he was, laying up there in a four-bed ward, on bed rest, not knowing what was going on. There I was, his wife and private nurse, visiting him until they had to kick me out, and trying my best to break the stringent rules to get my kids in to see their dad. At this hour of uncertainty, they needed to see him and have some assurance that he was coming home soon.

They decided to do a spinal tap and told the nurses to make sure he stayed on his back, logrolling for the necessary number of hours. This meant most of the night for him. In the morning, when I returned to discuss the night's events with him, I was told that they never checked the sight of the spinal tap. I was furious. My husband could have been leaking spinal fluid and they wouldn't have known.

Next, it was time for him to go for the nerve conduction test. He went for part of it and was told to come to the lab the next day at one o'clock to finish it. They said I could come also. I couldn't get there due to work. Phil waited and waited. This was typical. Patients were lining the halls, like shoppers in a deli line waiting for their number to be called. Finally, with no test done, he returned to his room. There was no explanation and no further testing done. It was just never completed. When I was able to look in his chart a few days later, it said it had been done! Our nightmare with the VA was just beginning. In previous times, whenever he experienced dizziness or other symptoms that brought him to the emergency room, they would always dismiss him with the same diagnosis.

"Stress."

I began to talk to the lonely elderly man across the room from Phil. He was hospitalized because he had a stroke. I didn't see a walker or wheelchair around his bed. My nursing instinct began to take over.

"Are you able to walk?"

"Yes, but they never get me out of this bed." He replied, wearing his frustration on his face where a smile used to be.

The man just laid there, trapped in the bed, with the television on day after day. When Phil was able to get around, he used to roll his wheelchair over to his roommate and challenge him to a game of checkers. I had too much on my mind with Phil and the kids to do any advocacy for that man. A couple of weeks after Phil was discharged, I saw the man's name on the obituary page. My distrust for the VA was growing.

The doctors ordered an EKG. When I was reading his chart the day before his discharge, I found that it had never been done. I challenged the head nurse, who just happened to see the order slip laying on the desk days after the orders had been written. She scheduled a last-minute EKG. All the tests were coming back negative.

Phil was looking for encouragement in any form he could get. One morning on his breakfast tray there was a little card with a scripture on it. He was so happy for that word he called to tell me.

"When you pass through the waters you shall not drown. When you walk through the fire, you shall not burn, neither shall the flame kindle upon you." Whatever his affliction was, he was persuaded he was going to beat it.

Our fourteenth anniversary was coming up that weekend and they were done testing him. Two weeks in the place was enough and we all wanted him home. I confronted the doctor.

"I think my husband can come home this weekend. There's nothing new going on or scheduled for him."

"Permission for his discharge has to be granted by the Chief of staff." He replied.

I was livid once again. Some haughty administrator sitting downstairs in his office didn't know my husband from Adam. I knew how the VA was great for dragging things out and as far as I was concerned, my husband wasn't going to sit in that place beyond Friday. It was Thursday. It was Memorial Day weekend, and it was going to be our anniversary. I stormed downstairs to the administrative offices.

"I want to speak to the Chief of Staff."

"Who are you?" The girl in the tweed pencil skirt questioned me.

"I am the wife of a patient you have upstairs, and I am a registered nurse. There is no reason for him to stay here this weekend and I want him discharged."

"The Chief is in a meeting. Can you come back?"

"No, I'll stay here and wait for him, thank you."

After a long while, the doctor came strolling nonchalantly out of his office, stretched out his introductory hand to me, inviting me inside. I spoke my complaint. In no uncertain terms was my husband staying in this hospital, uselessly, for the weekend. The short military doctor didn't give me much trouble. Our conversation broke through the red tape of the bureaucracy and Phil was allowed to come home the next day.

The MRI results came back negative after being read by the radiologists at both VA hospitals. Once again, they were telling Phil that his symptoms were all subjective. Being a nurse, I was acquainted with some of the various doctors in the city. I knew that the neurologist was a renowned expert on Multiple sclerosis and had written books on the subject. I had personal contact with him when working on the rehab floor at university Hospital and I knew he was personable as well as reputable. I was able to get an appointment at the nearby clinic. That day I had to be with the kids, and we decided I didn't have to go with Phil. I wish I had. That's when the boom fell, and I wasn't there with him. He took the MRI films from the VA with him. The doctor had his residents and interns with him that day. He put the films up on the board, looked at them, and proceeded to speak as he pointed to specific areas.

"Mr. Hansen, you have multiple sclerosis. Do you see these areas that are darker? These are lesions and this indicates that you've had this for a least ten years." Phil came home and reported the visit to me, telling me the thing we had feared. Emotions imploded within each of us as imaginations or our unknown future began to overwhelm us. The diagnosis of MS intruded our lives. Everything that wasn't already falling upside down and inside out was about to. With a sick husband who could no longer work, the demanding landlord, and boxes surrounding us, I ran to God. Tanya, Chris and Michael wanted to know where we were going to live, and I had no idea. Life was slamming doors in our faces left and right.

We began to argue more. We didn't know how to cope with all the pressure. I was unsure if the pressure would trigger the post-traumatic stress disorder in Phil and bring back flashbacks from Vietnam. I knew it had to do with an inability to cope when the stress came on. He was scared too but he couldn't tell me. He exhibited it in different ways, like being impatient. One morning we had another argument. He said he was going to the post office. My parents happened to come over. We visited. They left. Phil did not come home. Finally, there was a call. He was on his way to the VA hospital in Augusta, Maine, at least ten hours away. He told me he left a letter under the pillow. The pages of yellow legal paper were filled with shocking words that stabbed me in the heart.

"We need to work things out better. Our marriage is falling apart and maybe I'll be home by the end of summer. There are some signed checks here to help you take care of the family."

There were five checks. Horror gripped my heart as this unfounded surprise tore through me. He was gone to Maine. Why on earth had he chosen Maine? Why so far away? Most of all, how could he dare leave the kids and I sitting on boxes just days before we had to get out of there, not knowing where we were going? Inside of me, the anger churned like a tiny rumble that was about to explode into a huge earthquake.

I had to sit the kids down and tell them that daddy had left. How could he put them through this? Their security was blown enough!

"Daddy is gone on a trip to try to get help at the VA." My lips quivered and I felt faint before I finished my stoic attempt to keep them from being afraid. I started to cry. Did my kids have to take care of their mother now too? My daughter reassured me that God was in charge, and we needed to pray. We joined hands and prayed for daddy to come home.

A few hours later, a woman we had met at the local park called and told me about revival meetings going on at a church in the inner city that night. I told her what had happened. She gave me the name of the evangelist, along with his number and admonished me to call him. Desperate, I phoned this stranger and told him our plight.

"I'm worried that Phil will get in an accident or attempt suicide." I was worried that Vietnam would catch up to him again and something terrible would happen.

"Come tonight and bring a picture of Phil." He advised. His voice was assuring and confident. The kids and I went to the very loud service. The organ blared, the women wore fancy hats, and people waved their cardboard fans back and forth, pushing the hot air right, then left. Many got up and told testimonies of what God had done in their life. My children seemed to enjoy the music and all the praises. I just cried and prayed. They called a prayer line, and I brought the picture with me. He laid his hands on the picture and prayed for Phil.

"God is going to change Phil's heart and he is going to turn around and come home." He spoke as if he was so sure of the outcome. I had been praying that God would draw Phil to his bible and convict him to return home.

The day was long and draining. When the kids and I got in the door the beeping of the answering machine called us to its attention. The voice at the other end was that of the very tired one we had been praying for. The time of the call was the exact time of the prayer line at the church. He called back.

"I want you to know that I love you all. I've been reading my bible since I arrived at this hotel near Augusta. I'm sorry. While I was reading, I realized that I can't honor God and stay away. I'm coming home tomorrow."

I reminded him of the faithfulness of God once again, as we had prayed for him that night. God always won. Why didn't we learn and stop fighting him? Thanks to his faithfulness in our lives, the children were able to speak to their dad before they went to bed. Because of that, we were able to rest our heads on our pillows and sleep in peace that night. We were becoming the people we had often visited. Life took a strange unexplainable turn. Phil was about to become the homebound.

Chapter 15:
On the Road Again

As the days marched on, I started to understand a little more clearly what was going on with Phil. I could feel the pain, desperation, and loneliness within him that was just beginning. His legs hurt him. Then they were numb. He had dizzy episodes where he felt the room spinning. The headaches were foreboding. He was dropping things. I also felt remorse for being so impatient and short with him and assuming he was just conjuring up the fatigue. It wouldn't be the last time I felt this kind of remorse.

Since he was unable to work and we had rent that had to be paid, someone had to be the breadwinner. I tried working extra days on my job as a public health nurse. The office was only five minutes away, so I could squeeze little trips home between patients to check on things. I would take my paperwork home so I could try to maintain work and keep control over the home front. This was before the computers came to work with us. My job mileage multiplied on our little Cavalier. The stress began to build. Our world was falling apart. It was rolling like tumbleweed with no specific direction and often getting stuck on countless new obstacles that we had to confront. I found that I could no longer work the extra days and keep my sanity. I couldn't be in two places at once. When I was at the other end of the county, there was no way I could be at home if my family needed me. I cut back to a two-day work week. I still had to work. My supervisors were very understanding. The local Catholic church brought us food weekly. Our landlord was getting anxious. He knew our circumstances and he was trying to get us to buy the house. He wanted to raise the rent. We couldn't handle that. We couldn't afford to purchase the house. We didn't know what to do.

When I was at work, the children became their father's caregiver. They were each developing a new compassion and responsibility. This was a huge undertaking and unfair for them at the ages of twelve, eleven and seven. We did what we had to do to exist. The father that used to come home from work, change his clothes, and go play football in the street with them, rallying all the neighbor kids, could no longer participate. Now he was home all the time and sleeping most of it. Some days he'd try to shoot baskets into the basketball hoop on the garage. Eventually, he had to do it from a sitting position on a folding chair. His legs couldn't be depended upon like they once could.

Before those days, when I came home from work, Phil always had a team effort going in the kitchen. I was forbidden to enter the secret domain where my family would be brewing up some scrumptious, savory smelling concoction to surprise and please me.

"You go get comfortable in the living room and leave the dinner to us."

Some nights, they even served me by candlelight. They took such joy in this. After dinner, I became the queen who was ordered to retreat to my favorite chair and put my feet up. I was told in no uncertain terms that dishes were off limits to me. My children were learning to serve, and they loved it. Their father was teaching them this priceless lesson. From my post in the chair, I heard their young little voices under direction of their dad's deeper articulation as they organized the kitchen for cleaning. What we didn't know was that someday in the not-too-distant future, they would have to use all that he taught them in order to serve him. In such a short time, like an unexpected wild wind, this changed too.

There was no more coming home to the music of my little family of servants in the kitchen. Uncertainty and confusion greeted me at the door and instability threatened our future. This metamorphosis was already beginning to crush us.

While Phil was in the hospital, I was going through personal anguish I had never known. The attic schoolroom was newly refinished with a skylight. One afternoon I climbed the stairs to the attic in tears, shaking my fist at the sky. Crying out to God with all the fears and frustrations, my anger bounced off the walls and back into my heart. It was that day that I called God a liar, which I knew deep inside was not the truth. My faith was shaken severely for the first time since becoming a Christian twelve years ago. If anyone ever asked me if I thought I'd one day call God a liar, I would have thought that was an impossibility. It was also the day that I asked God to prove that he really existed.

For the next seven years, God did exactly that, yet not in the way that I would have expected. He proved himself repeatedly. I had asked him a year before that to make me a woman of faith. If I had known what it would take, I might never have asked. Before the glory, there had to be suffering. The servant is not greater than the Master. I might have been Christian for twelve years, but I was in kindergarten again. Our lives were shattered. What we were to learn in the next few months showed us that we needed the very God whom I had called a liar. We weren't going to make it without him.

Chapter 16:
The Cabin

Seventeen doctors later, Phil's exposure to Agent Orange had finally caught up with him, though the VA was reluctant to admit it. The neuro doctor saw the lesions and confirmed the diagnosis. He also said that Phil had it for a least ten years, which coincided with his return from the war. He also had Nystagmus when he came home, which was the twitching of the eyes that my sister-in-law had told me he used to joke about. I found out more after tedious phone calls into his past trips to emergency rooms in Cooperstown and Rochester before I knew him. He had been having bouts of fevers of unknown origin, and vague, difficult to diagnose, symptoms that could have been indicative of early MS.

I agonized before God and pleaded with him to let us know where we could go, since our time to stay in that house was ending. I sat on the boxes piled high in the living room, looking around in quiet desperation. I was fearful and uncertain. One of the children came to me.

"Mommy, where are we going to go?"

"I don't know, but God does." I replied, sounding like a giant of faith but feeling like a weak, whimpering kitten.

Kneeling at the couch in the middle of the afternoon, between boxes and crying, I prayed.

"We'll take anywhere but the street or the Rescue Mission." I pleaded.

The words 'bible camp' came into my spirit. As sure as I know my name, I knew He was announcing the answer to my prayer. I jumped up, announcing that God had given us a place to go. It was perfect. The kids loved it and since we'd been there before it wasn't a strange place. It was on Lake Ontario so there would be a breeze off the lake to keep Phil cool since the MS was exacerbated by heat and humidity. It was only $17 per week to stay in a cabin. I would be able to transport to work although the commute would be forty-five minutes one-way. We always loved camping, the outdoors, and the slower pace that it gave us. Less stress would help. If only our marriage would stabilize. Perhaps in a peaceful setting we could work on it. God knew we needed the calm setting. With our lives going down the tubes, our future loomed like a dark wall of uneasiness before us. We were losing communication daily.

On June 14, 1992, our Pastor came to our house with the entire youth group and a couple of trucks. He and the teens loaded the bulk of the heavy stuff; piano, furniture and appliances, into the trucks to be taken to his mother's barn where it would be stored until we had a home. Phil, the kids, and I loaded our two cars with what we thought we'd need to survive until the next move. He couldn't lift heavy things anymore. It was a hot, muggy July afternoon. Woven in with the physical demand of moving was the bittersweet pill of leaving our home of almost four years and facing unknown paths ahead. No other choices were ours that day, and my heart ached as I watched the pained face of my husband trying to lift anything. He was trying to have some control over the life he was losing, trying to maintain some pride in man's strength as he directed us with what we should do.

The tail end of the afternoon brought thunderclouds and rain. The children were saying good-bye to their friends on the street. The last truckload was gone and with very little strength left, we lugged the heavy tools and items from our basement across the street to our neighbor's house. They agreed to keep some of our things until we could find a place to live. We would never forget this place. It was the place where our lives had changed unexpectedly forever.

Looking like hillbillies again, replete with everything from television to pets, we made the journey to the water trying desperately to pretend this was just another regular vacation. Phil was still able to drive, so he took the kids in one car, and I took the one of the cats in the other. We said good-bye to the big white house, leaving behind the octagonal picnic table that we loved, because we had no way to carry it.

"We'll leave it for the neighbors." Phil decided.

Cats and kids in the car, we drove off. As I drove, I wondered if the piano that Phil had surprised me with would be any good after spending forced time in someone's barn. How long would we have to be without a home of our own? The rush hour traffic was strangling and Mr. Sparky, our cat, moved back and forth, front to back, hyperventilating in panic from the long car ride. I prayed and sang, hoping the cat wouldn't cause an accident. I had to stop and drop my wedding gown off with our friends. I was not about to leave that to be victimized by the mildew of the barn for a few weeks. Little did I know at that time that a few weeks would turn out to be three months.

Finally, arriving at the camp, we checked in. Our two weeks reservations went up to the beginning of August. After that, another family was scheduled to come in. At the time, we were so tired, we just rolled with the punches, assuming that when August came, we'd just be able to move into another cabin. We began to work again, finding places for sleeping bags, two cats, two kittens, rabbit and cage. My eyes were sore and swollen from crying back at the house while the youth group packed our belongings. Phil used his muscles and sweat as the MS ebbed in the late afternoon heat. The breeze of the lake was refreshingly splendorous as we unpacked to the sounds of the waves only thirty feet from our cabin.

The little porch of the one-room home served as our kitchen and pantry. Underneath the red Formica table, we stowed our boxes of food. This is where the famous box of never-ending granola lived. Our children remember that to this day. They had their fill of granola that summer! The screened-in area would work fine for us on rainy days when we couldn't use the outside picnic table. Inside was another story. The dimensions of the cabin fit in the category of a very tiny house. There were five of us, one dresser, one single bed, and two sets of bunk beds. Two small windows and a back door facilitated air passage as I worked hurriedly to ready the beds, knowing that Phil was long overdue for his much-needed rest. Narrow, two-inch thick mattresses covered the springs. I arranged the room, pushing one set of bunks against the wall, and the other set against the end of the first. Phil could not climb, so I took the single bed and pushed it up against the side of the bunk closest to the front door. I would take the bottom and Phil could have the outside access next to me on the single twin. I covered the skimpy mattresses with sheets trying to give the place a woman's touch and somehow turn cramped into cozy.

Next, I had to set up the fan. This was no Holiday Inn and there was no air conditioning here. Hot nights would not benefit Phil. Fighting mosquitoes probably would make the nights long enough. The fan went up on top of the dresser. Each of the kids got a drawer to themselves. I set two boxes on top of each other, open ends facing outwards.

This was our dresser. Fortunately, on the campground was a laundry room, public phones, a mess hall, a chapel, and a first aid station. The bathroom was a short walk away in a different building. Finally unpacked, the kids took to the lake and Phil crashed on the bed. I sat outside, stared at the lake, and cried some more.

The next day came with restored energy and new anticipation. Our material things were secure, and we wouldn't have to pack and move so we were free to wander. The silence between Phil and I spoke volumes regarding the change that had forced its way into our relationship. Tension in that silence seemed to wait like a lion in hiding, about to attack at the slightest provocation.

During this, there was good news. The kid's bible camp was going to start that day. The ages of the eligible children lined up with the ages of our three. This would involve supervised activities with other children, bible contests, cookouts, campfires, and other fun things. The couple in charge of the camp knew Phil because the husband worked at the Rescue Mission. They very graciously made arrangements so our children could all attend camp at a rate we could afford, and the kids were in. They were very happy, and it helped get their minds off the circumstances that were gravely bearing down on us. Once again, I thanked God that he has opportunities hidden for us, even in adversity. In the center of the storm, he had hidden this jewel for us. It was waiting for us at the camp. He loved our children, and his fatherly characteristics rang true that summer. When we felt less adequate to be parents, and we felt too weak to have the strength to bolster each other, God came through with strength for our children.

Chapter 17:
Never Without Trials

Two full weeks of adventure and R&R went quickly for all of us in our little cabin. Days of tumultuous rain forced us to cook on our hibachi and dine on the little screened-in porch. As the rain fell, cabin fever became contagious. Irritability flourished, like the relentless buzzing of an unwanted fly. Everyone was wearing their nerves on their sleeves. There were moments of solitude and reflection. Often, on nice days, I would walk alone up to the top of my favorite place at the camp. This was the hill that hovered over the great lake. The vantage from this precipice granted me the pleasure of long reflective moments as I watched the waves come in and pound the rocky shore. The awesome power of the water always helped me focus on God. The scriptures refer to Him as having the voice as the 'sound of many waters.' I named my adopted place, "The Lord's Hill."

It was there that I went alone to cry, pray, and seek God's presence. I wondered what our future would hold. I imagined we had a house on that hill. In the backyard there was the thick company of evergreen woods. The trees stood, like guardian angels, letting the wind move through them in gentle hushing sounds. Occasionally, a cottontail would hop out and display himself as I walked, prayed, and imagined. The breeze up there was always restorative and reassuring. The Lord's Hill became my oasis.

Though Phil was unable to swim anymore, which he had enjoyed so much previously, he rigged up a way to get wet. He anchored a lawn chair in the rocks where he could sit in the water, pant legs rolled up, sunglasses on, and allow those waves to encircle him on his home-made throne. Cool splashes refreshed him and kept the heat from causing an MS flare-up.

He and I would go for short walks down by the cabin or lay out on a blanket in the shade. We read a book that might help us work out our marriage problems. It was about opposites attacking each other. Sometimes we'd watch the kids fishing. Sometimes we'd all watch the carp swimming in the shallow water under a small bridge. There was a nuclear energy plant less than a mile away that crushed the real idea of rusticating in the wilderness. Some friends would come to visit. We'd cook out and have s'mores around the fire.

One day, our daughter decided to explore unknown territory with her friend. There was an abandoned house across the road. The overgrowth didn't stop them from going to get the berries growing closer to the house. They feasted on the juicy treats, then returned to camp. The next day, she awoke with a case of poison ivy so bad that her eyes were swollen shut. I took a walk to the first aid cabin and found God's provision for us once again. There was a kind doctor from West Virginia visiting. He just happened to have some prednisone with him, which is exactly what Tanya needed. He gave it to me, free of charge. We were in adversity, but God was working out all the details. Michael also caught a mild case of poison ivy that year. Mosquito bites were plenteous. Luckily, Phil remained impervious to those visitors. Chris was winning the bible verse competition contest and we all got to watch the kids compete.

Our rental time came to an end, and someone else was scheduled to move into our cabin. We tried to get another cabin since we still had no idea where we would go next.

None were available. We had to be out by Sunday. Money was scarce. We didn't know what we would do. I had been searching for homes in three counties to see if there was someone who would rent to us. I had my real estate license, so I was able to check homes with access to the lockboxes. Nothing had come up. I wasn't selling houses either, because I couldn't afford the yearly $400 fees to be on the Board of Realtors.

That rainy Saturday, we started out very early and began our search to find our next shelter. We checked the campground across the street. It was nice. It had little cabins with more than one room, air conditioners, and beds with sheets. A maid cleaned the rooms daily. There was a refrigerator, stove and sofas, all nestled within the pines for $300 per week. To us it would have been like moving to a Manhattan penthouse, but we couldn't afford the fee. That was precisely all money we had left.

Onward we went, deciding on the way that an efficiency apartment would suit us well until we could find a home. We didn't think about the possibility that we wouldn't be able to afford it. We were desperate. We went to several places and found there were no vacancies, or they were too expensive. Phil was getting more exhausted as the hours dragged by. I was getting frustrated. The kids were getting irritable. The rain kept falling and it was gray. We had to be out the next day. Where would we go? Phil suggested we stop at a mall for a drink. The gloomy sky was relentless.

It was there, in the mall at the center of the food court, that I lost it. Holding my emotions in was beyond me. I began to cry. It was already five o'clock. Our chances of finding anything were mighty slim. I couldn't make the simple decision of what to get the kids to drink. The sobs came harder and louder.

"Maybe they'll let us stay in the mall." I cried to my husband, wanting so badly to lean on him for strength when I knew I was the one that had to be the strength for the family. Once again, his faith was stronger than mine and he took us through.

"We will go back to the first camp we found. You need the break, and we will just have to trust God." His proclamation was decisive.

"We won't have any money left!" I protested. He reiterated.

"We will have to step out and trust God to help us. We are told to take no thought for tomorrow."

I was too weary to fight and had no other ideas. So, I conceded, and we made our way back to the place in the pines and booked our cabin for one week with our last $300. Tired as we were, we still had to return to our first place and finish packing so we could be out in the morning.

Sunday morning came and the nomads hit the trail again, crossing the street to our penthouse. The kids were never upset. Everything was a new adventure with them. They met other kids there and rode bikes around the paved circle. The air conditioning was a wonderful reprieve for Phil. Real beds with clean sheets and a kitchen to cook in were glorious to me. I tried to trust God and kept pushing the fear to the back of my mind. What were we to do now with no money until the next month came, bringing the next social security disability check? We had been denied food stamps since we didn't have a permanent residence in that county. A friendly Christian soup kitchen became our source for groceries. Day-old bagels and whatever else they gave us became our staples.

The following Wednesday evening, we attended church as usual. We hadn't been there the previous weekend. Someone we didn't know walked up to us.

"God told me to give you this." He stated, handing us an envelope.

He had no idea of what we had just been through the previous weekend. In the envelope was $350! God's faithfulness proved true again. He had heard of us and felt led in prayer to help us. I just sat down and cried. It felt like 'cry' was my middle name during that stage of life. I thanked the man and thanked God once again for his faithfulness to us. We didn't even have to ask. God just knew what we needed and provided it through another of His children. He was rewarding my husband's faithfulness and teaching me to lean on Him.

Our week in the pines went quickly and we relaxed greatly, but we only had the palace for a week, so we were already questioning what would be next. We were close to a family from church. They had planned their vacation to Washington, DC. They came to us and asked if we'd like to move in and babysit their home while they were gone. Our kids got along great with their kids. These people were already holding my wedding gown and our beat-up pop-up camper. Considering the situation, we couldn't refuse this timely and gracious offer. The lady of the house even went the extra mile to make sure she filled the cupboards for us with things that we all liked. We felt like the royal family moving up to a real house with thicker mattresses and all the amenities of home. Again, God was providing. It was one step at a time. It reminded me of one of his promises in the Bible.

"As thou goes, the way shall be opened up, step by step before you."

That family showed genuine unselfish love for us. They were gone for a week. The summer was rolling by. What was next? Was this what it meant to walk by faith?

One night, before the first move even occurred, Phil had a dream about another friend from church. In the dream, he was telling Bill to keep his eye out for a house for us. After the dream, Phil saw him and told him about the dream.

"I don't know what this means, but last night I dreamt that you were supposed to look out for a house for us, so if you see anything, let us know."

He politely responded that he'd do so. There we were, months later, looking for another place of shelter. Bill lived in a town called Cato, not too far from our church. One day during our stay, he called and wanted to talk to Phil.

"My next-door neighbor just went through a divorce. He's been living alone in his big house and he's hardly home. I told him about you, and he decided to offer his place for you to live as long as you need. He has made a loft over his garage, and he will sleep there."

At the end of the week, we packed our things and moved into the big house in Cato. Bill had eight children, and many were boys. Our boys played football in the street with them. Across the street was another home-schooling family. They had girls. My daughter got to be friends with them easily.

The big colonial house had a unique character. It spoke loudly of loneliness, unfinished business, and interrupted lives. The house where a married couple and a little boy had once lived was now occupied by the man of the house. Through the large front door, we entered a spacious vestibule. To the left was the living room, cold and carpeted in part with a shag rug. The back wall of that room was glass. We could see the owner's giant husky outside. To the right was a dining room which adjoined the kitchen. It looked like the remodeling had abruptly stopped. The microwave was the only working cooking apparatus. Off the kitchen was a small outside area with vines overtaking it. Once, it must have been a nice place to relax. To the right of the kitchen was at the garage with the loft where the owner would reside. Upstairs, via the massive staircase in the middle of the vestibule, we found the bedrooms. There was the master bedroom complete with a king-sized waterbed, and two smaller rooms. Mattresses on the floor indicated that the two boys could share the one room and Tanya had the last room-the one with the washing machine in it. The bathroom had a life of its own. There, one would gingerly step, avoiding the hole in the floor. We could see the kitchen below and hear every word being spoken. The water pressure was weak, a good indication of why the bachelor pad was missing the sparkling cleaning the tub needed. I immediately attacked that tub, cleanser in hand. Even the abrasiveness of the cleanser wasn't enough to scrub off the layer of grime the had accumulated. I shuddered at the thought of taking showers in that thing, then I thanked God that there was a shower and that we had a roof over our head.

The whole house was dark. Sunlight had very little opportunity to filter in. Shadows formed a holding place for the constant chill. It was a good thing it was not winter. Phil was still walking but had to use a walker on occasion. With difficulty and help, he could make it upstairs to the bedroom. With help he could also make it out of the waterbed in the morning. It felt terribly awkward to be sleeping in this stranger's bed, even though he was willing to give it up. I always felt like hidden eyes were watching us. The kids thought it was an adventure, as usual. Since we went to the same church together, the kids already knew each other. They spent time playing football, swimming, or exploring the little town. Often, they would go to the cemetery to play hide and seek behind the ancient, whitewashed monuments.

In the meantime, I was attempting to put my real estate license to work. I had taken the course and obtained the license in the city before everything fell apart. The multiple listing service was just coming on the computer, and it was exclusive thing. I was still signed up under a broker, so I still used my opportunity to search for a house for us. When I found a vacant house, I'd call the owner and ask if they might rent or hold the mortgage with option to buy. All I knew was that we had to find a home. We couldn't stay in that house forever.

One day my mother called me.

"There's a house in Weedsport for rent. It says it's a historical house. You might want to check it out."

We went to see it. I found out that the little house was ancient. It even went back to the days when a road ran between the hills behind it where people would travel to the next town. Next door was a decrepit mansion that a three-member family lived in. I learned that back in the 1800s, the old inn used to have kitchen quarters in the back, separate from the house. I found that in those days, the kitchen quarters were always separate for fear of fires occurring and causing damage to the main inn. The little house had been put on rollers at one time much later and rolled onto the property next door. Since that time, it had stood as a single residency and at one time functioned as a dairy.

The people renting it were headed south. They had just married in their later years and wanted to get away from the harsh central NY winters. They were very kind. There was a huge barn, and beyond the barn was a field and stream. The barn was bulging with treasures. There was depression glass, books, ancient wooden ironing boards, and all kinds of things. We rented it for five hundred dollars a month. It was very small. The floors leaned towards the back of the house. With a good pair of roller skates, a body could roll right through the house and out the back door. It didn't matter to us. The idea of having our own place to live in was exhilarating.

Tanya got the room off the kitchen that barely had heat. Chris and Mike had to share the tiny middle room. We found a mouse hole in the wall. That was unsettling to me, along with the lack of cupboards in the kitchen. Doing the dishes was a chore that presented a challenge, since there was no counter space. It required the use of a TV table to set the clean dishes up to drain.

In the center of the long living room was a huge Vermont Castings wood stove. We had homes in the past with fireplaces and wood stoves, so this made the place cozy and warm. As Phil began to experience the numbness in his hands and feet, and his judgement began to wane, the wood stove became a dangerous thing to have.

One morning, he walked outside in the snow without realizing he was barefooted. He had less feeling in his hands and fingers as well. He always insisted on being the one to stoke the fire. His hands got small burns on them repeatedly because he couldn't feel the heat of the stove. A friend of ours heard about it and gave him a pair of blue welding gloves to keep future burns and blisters away. He was stubborn though and didn't wear them.

Getting wood to keep us warm also became a trial. After making several phone calls, I finally found someone to help. The local American Legion donated a cord of wood to us and delivered it one Saturday morning. Because some pieces were damp, Phil had a habit of leaning them up against the warm, burning stove to dry out. He also placed some on top of the stove. One night, shortly after everyone was tucked into bed, I smelled smoke. Our little bedroom was right off the living room. I opened the door and faced a wood stove with flames on top. I grabbed the teakettle of water that I kept close and poured it over the sizzling flames. That was the last time the damp wood got close to the stove.

That year, 1993, was the year from Hell. Phil was still able to walk with support. He would go jogging through the back roads of town with the assist of a ski pole he had picked up at the local thrift shop. Running from block to block, holding the ski pole above his head in a horizontal position for balance, he'd progress, not caring what people thought. He was still taking the risk of getting hurt, and he was tiring faster than ever.

In the winter, he took our three energetic children behind the barn and up into the hills. They carried their sleds so they could still experience the outdoor times with dad. Many times since, I have passed that place, looked up to those hills, and regretted that I was too busy to go with them on those trips. My essential wife and mother duties frequently kept me from having those memories. They would come home, hang up their snowsuits, and let me serve them a cup of hot cocoa. Phil collapsed in his chair and fell asleep.

Phil wanted to get a dog for Chris. It was a family dog, but it was to be known as Chris's. I worked with a nurse who raised huskies. We contacted them and went to see them. Chris chose the one with the blue eyes and named her "Lightning." She was a beautiful dog. Sometimes it caused stress. Phil would get upset if the dog wasn't walked when he thought it should be. He became demanding with Chris about it. Despite that, the pup gave many smiles to the family at a time when it was needed.

PJ, the white rabbit, belonged to Tanya. When PJ got to the point where his leg was hurt somehow, the vet said we should but him to sleep. Tanya didn't want to let it go, so I had to be the nurse to the rabbit, bandaging its leg and feeding it lettuce by hand. It couldn't hop over to get his food anymore. Eventually, he succumbed.

Incidents of verbal abuse were escalating. Phil's words became terse and hurtful. At Christmas, he decided to have a student from Teen Challenge join us. This was ok with me, since this was the kind of thing we used to do in the old Rescue Mission days. We believed in helping and encouraging the less fortunate. The kids waited to open their gifts while he went thirty miles into Syracuse to pick up the young man. We waited impatiently. Finally, I called him.

"Where are you?" I demanded, upset that he had been gone so long.

"I'm at your grandmother's. We decided to stop by and we're having a cup of coffee." I was really upset about the delay.

"The kids are waiting to open their presents and you decide to stop at my grandmothers! Give her my greetings and come home!"

Phil's whole demeanor changed towards me. I couldn't sort out why he was acting as if he hated me. I was doing everything I could for him and the family. I was trying to manage our crashing world and dealing with the heartache of all the changes. As I tried feverishly in every way to take care of it all, his anger and new mean attitude toward me only seemed to increase. His judgement was changing, and he wouldn't acknowledge it. He was fighting every step of the way for his control.

He refused to give up the financial obligations and bounced checks consecutively as if they were going out of style. Money was tight enough without us having to pay for bounced checks. He kept ordering cassette tapes of all kinds of music. I assumed that was probably because listening to the music was about all he could do any more. When I tried to speak to him about these things, it only served to fuel his anger.

He wouldn't stop driving. One night he was picking the kids up from a youth activity. Chris was getting into the car, but his leg was still dangling out the door. I was thankful he had heavy boots on, because Phil started backing the car over his toe.

"Dad! Stop! You're starting to run over my toe!"

I never doubted that an angel protected our son that night. I told Phil he would have to get his driving checked. We found out that the Motor vehicle department would test him and tell us how he did. Phil gladly accepted the challenge, only to say goodbye to his last bit of freedom when the brownie informed us that he was no longer a safe driver. They gave him a piece of paper that stated that it was because of the MS that he could no longer drive. He stashed it in the glove compartment.

The more he lost the more devastated he became, and the angrier he became with everyone. At that point, we had regular counseling appointments with our pastor. It was hard for me to sort out what was the real Phil and what might have been the MS affecting his mentation. All I knew was the struggling to do everything, trying to encourage him, constant arguing, and emotional abuse was becoming overwhelming and degrading.

One morning, we were in the garage with two of our children. We were doing the chore everyone hated, sorting recyclables. Phil was not in a good mood. He challenged me about something, and I retorted quickly.

"I'll slap you in the face." He snapped.

"You certainly will not!" I responded.

Just as soon as I'd said it, he reached across the bags of cans and slapped me hard across the face. In my instant reaction of anger and hurt, I herded the kids to the car and left the house. I went to a local park, crying hysterically. Hopeless, and feeling trapped, I walked around the park with the kids.

"I can't allow this behavior to continue! If I allow it, it will happen again!" I told them through the stinging tears. We returned home and I kept my distance from my husband. After fifteen years of going through all kinds of things in our marriage, I thought it was going to come to an end. I was beginning to be frightened daily. The constant barrage of fiery darts of condemnation from him was wearing me down. He was upset because he couldn't do much of the homeschooling anymore. I gave him some assignments, but his memory and judgement only impeded the progress of the classes. He was angry about that too. I loved my husband, but I couldn't go on living like that. Sleep came harder every night.

One night the digits on the alarm clock stared back at me. It was ten twenty-three. It had been an early night. Everyone was asleep. I sat up in bed, staring into space. The day's exhaustion was catching up to me. Every cell in my body throbbed with the fatigue. Every throb chanted mercilessly.

"Sleep, sleep, sleep."

The hardness of the cold wooden headboard behind me reminded me that I couldn't give in to the sleep just yet. The place where my sacrum touched the mattress was aching. My eyelids were growing heavy, as if tiny weights were forcing them down.

At last, the small house was still. The long-awaited time of refuge returned. The time of day when silence soothed the soul had come. Except for an occasional car passing on the road, stillness bathed me like a rich cloak of comfort and warmth. The faint scent of recently applied hair conditioner permeated the silence, a pleasant intrusion. The nights of perfume and candles had become extinct. Licking my dry lips, I tasted traces of toothpaste. It reminded me of a time when even my lips weren't lonely.

I stared for a long moment at the face of my sleeping spouse. I reached out to stroke his face. It was cool. How I wished the touches I gave him could assure him of my love for him. We had been through a lot. That included the earlier days of our marriage when he went through the PTSD, sleeping with his Army knife under our mattress and trying not to be afraid during the flashbacks. I fantasized that each stroke of my fingers across his temple would echo a million times into his brain.

"I love you."

The new red scar on his forearm was showing. It was just another burn he had acquired from the wood stove. He hardly ever noticed the burns or the cuts. The question forced its way into my weary mind.

"Why does he have to go through this?"

As always, I found no answer. The flowered pillowcase moved with his breathing. I wanted it to move forever.

"Don't think too much right now." I told myself. I tried to write my feelings in my journal. My gaze kept shifting from the paper to his face. The endearment was strong, lying beneath the recent mountains of arguing and tears. Like layers of transparent onion skin that could be peeled away, the pungency and fervor of life still existed somewhere deep below. The desires, passion, and dreams were still intact. The love stayed preserved within my heart for him.

Resolving to begin anew with God's grace when morning came, I was again forced to listen to the exhaustion. I could hear my snoring son. My lower back was aching for mercy, to lie down so the pain would stop. I found myself staring again, growing numb from it all. The green leaves of the plant caught my eye and appeared to move ever so slowly, in tune with the calls of sleep from my cells. Too exhausted to pursue anything more, I gazed again at the man beside me. There was a world of hurts that I wanted to take away every day. Instead, I failed. Abandoning the pen, and reaching to turn off the light, my heart gave a whimper. My only assurance was that God had heard the cry. I crawled beneath the burgundy satin covers and embraced him. I wanted to be near him forever. I wanted to become him-one, like it was intended to be. Always wanting, I drifted asleep. This was my time.

Phil's twenty-one-year-old son came to live with us for a while. We were all excited to see him and have him with us. We loved him like crazy. He is good looking and talented. He was coming from Colorado. At first, he slept on the couch. Later, we made a room for him up in the attic. How enduring he was to go through all of that. He drew caricatures of all of us. He got a job shoveling snow for an apartment complex. He taught the kids to dance to the "Boot Scootin' Boogie." He was the western influence.

Soon my children were acting like they were all twenty-one. He even got boots from the local western store. I wish I could remember more details about his stay with us. I was so caught up in the changes that were going on and all I had to do that it was emotionally paralyzing.

Eventually, Tom got another job at the mini mart down the street. From there, he went on to Florida to live near his sister and grandmother. He told me years later that his dad told him he had to leave. Sadly, I don't remember any of this happening.

One spring day I decided to go for a morning walk. The sun was warm against my face and the birds sang in symphony as I walked. My heart was heavy as my steps took me further from home. Despair propelled me forward, driving me faster. Oppression pulled my feet down. This dawn the family slept, and I took to the village streets. To where?

As I heard the business section of town, I could see that some residents had already begun to stir. Eighteen-wheelers shifted down and then roared up to the diesel pumps. The smell of coffee stirred my senses. My feet found their way into the small restaurant. I took a booth by myself across from God. I was determined that He would talk this morning. I was also determined to get some answers, or I would not go home.

So, there we sat, God and I, in the booth near the plate glass window that flaunted the view of one of New York State's major truck routes. I sipped my Mocha Java and began to talk. The silent conversation took place in my head and heart. He was silent as I whined on.

"How can I go on? How can I cope? I am so overwhelmed. MS has taken over my husband. It's not MS, it's 'Myself.' We fight constantly. Our home is falling apart.

144

He's bouncing checks every week. He's becoming abusive. How? How can I possibly go on?" I pleaded.

My relentless liturgy became inwardly frustrating. Where was my answer? When I finally felt that I had poured out my heart, my lips left the coffee cup and my eyes shifted above to the window. At that precise moment my answer came, silent, yet screaming before me. This eighteen-wheeler wasn't too late. As it rolled by, just for me, a rare moment was ordained by God, as if it had fallen out of heaven. Only a fool could have missed it. It glided by before my eyes. On the side of that truck, like a personal drive-in screen, the giant sign written in capital letters thundered into my heart.

"Grace."

He had spoken, and I knew it. God uses many ways of trying to speak to me. Peace flooded me. It was more overwhelming than the distress that had me in knots. Finishing the coffee, but no longer interested in it, I pushed the mug back on the table. I rose to my feet. Now faster, more determined, I held my head up and walked out. I knew without a doubt that no matter what, the grace of God would sustain me.

Chapter 18:
From Bad to Worse

Life was getting unbearable. Everything seemed to be getting worse. We sought out a counselor in the hopes that our marriage could be helped. One day, we were sitting in the overstuffed chairs in the counselor's office. I felt the blood rush to my head, followed by a terrible headache. I was bombinated by the verbal volleyball that bantered back and forth between us. This was supposed to be a Christian counselor whom a friend had referred us to. Every week we argued our way into his office in the historic Methodist church. Instead of allowing the man to work with us, we'd put on a display of emotional fireworks for the hour we were there, and then go home upset.

The inevitable week finally came after all the volatile appointments.

"Now we have to decide how you two can split up and still let the children be assured that it isn't their fault, and that they're still loved." The one who was supposed to help save our marriage told us the next step.

I left very angry. My stomach churned. I wanted to vomit due to the acquiescence of this guys' proposal to us. I was appalled. This so-called "Christian counselor" never brought up one word that belonged to God. Now he was telling us the only option was divorce. In my heart, I didn't want a divorce. I didn't know how I could keep going with all the verbal and emotional abuse and the pressure of having a sick husband and three children to care for.

Torn and desperate, I dropped Phil off at the house and sped away, applying the pressure of my life to the gas pedal. Driving further into the country on random back roads, crying so hard I could barely see, I pulled the car over on top of a hill by a corn field. The air smelled like dry corn stalks and rotting cabbage. With no one there except me, nature, and God, I cried out.

"God! I don't want a divorce! I just don't know what to do! I can't keep going if something doesn't change!"

Seconds after my plea, an enormous hawk flew out of nowhere and hovered low to the ground in the flattened corn field, next to the car. He glided around as if he knew I was there. It was as if he was bringing me a message. I had never witnessed such a close visit by one of these winged creatures and it took me by surprise. Immediately, the words filled my spirit, and I knew God was speaking to my heart.

"They that wait upon the Lord shall renew their strength. They shall mount up with wings as eagles. They shall run and not be weary, they shall walk and not faint."

I just had to hold on and trust that God knew what he was doing. A surge of assurance sprang into me, as if I had been injected with some supernatural steroid. I knew without a doubt that God had spoken once again. He is forever faithful. I thanked him, knowing that if He told me to wait, he would renew my strength and help us to go on. I turned around and found my way back home. When I arrived, Phil was more calm and pleasant than I had seen him in weeks. Little had I known, but when I left, he had rallied the kids in prayer, knowing in his heart, like me, that he didn't want a divorce either. God had heard us both praying separately, yet our hearts were one. He changed things again and we were given strength to endure.

Major choices soon confronted us again. The people that owned the house wanted it sold. We were given the first choice to buy. In my wild imagination, I dreamt of straightening the rolling floors, remodeling, and adding on until it was beautifully transformed. Looking back, I see a blatant example of how God knows what's best for us. My imagination was nowhere close to the reality that was ahead. We tried again to obtain a mortgage, to no avail. They refused to negotiate a land contract. Once again, the nomads were looking for a place to live, just one year after we had moved in. Did life always have to be so disheartening?

At that time, we had begun attending a church in nearby Auburn. We had become regular patrons at their food pantry. The children were making friends there. We decided to look for a place closer, in that small city. Ironically, I was born there. I had told someone that I'd never move there. The search began. Now we had Christopher's Husky. We had to find a place to rent that would allow pets again. I had to find a house that we could afford on our meager budget. Once again, I drove around everywhere in search for a home for my family. There was a difference this time. Phil's condition was worse. He couldn't even lift. His walking had grown more unstable. It was October and winter was coming. How could I move my family by myself? The overwhelming scenario pressed hard on me as the stress increased.

On one of my rides, I drove to a back road that ran behind the city. It was pretty out there. I thought when I discovered it that this would be a nice place to live but couldn't find a place available. Winter was coming. The odds seemed to point against us. No houses were available to rent, and I was afraid we were going to end up in an apartment and have to get rid of the pets. I prayed for God to answer. I prayed what I thought was an impossible prayer. I asked for a four-bedroom house with a good yard, not far from church. I also prayed for a place with a downstairs bathroom and master bedroom that I could get Phil into. I didn't think there would be much time before he wouldn't be able to get upstairs. I also prayed for a wood stove to help with the heat, rent no higher than five-hundred dollars, and a yard so we could keep the pets. It needed to be available when we had to be out of the house, which was November 15th. I searched the papers and one day found an ad for a compact four-bedroom house with a woodburning stove. I called the landlord. Surprisingly, the house was on that same road that I had fallen in love with! We drove out to the place. I wouldn't have noticed it because there was no sign on it.

The landlord walked us into the small place with a tiny front porch. The oak hardwood floors gleamed back at us from the dining room. The living room had a beautiful bay window that encompassed most of the wall, looking out on a yard that was over an acre. Little falls bubbled in the outlet from the lake that ran at the back edge of the property. Inside, the burgundy carpet set off the woodwork. The landlord bragged as he showed us what he had done to fix the place up. In the corner was a huge wood stove.

"It heats the whole place in the winter." He informed us.

The living room extended into an eat-in kitchen with hardwood floors and oak cupboards. Off the kitchen was a half-bath, where the laundry appliances fit. By that time my heart was pounding. This was too good to be true. My prayers were unfolding before my eyes. Then I looked off to the other side of the kitchen. There was a mauve colored master bedroom. God was doing it again! Despite my whining and complaining, doubts and fears, there was no shadow of turning with Him. A huge glassed-in porch ran the length of the back of the house, overlooking the outlet waters as the little rapids raced by. I held my breath and threw out the question.

"How much is the rent?" I said, timidly.

"Five-hundred dollars monthly." He stated.

I looked at Phil with big eyes. My heart pounded.

"We have to move in two weeks. We must be out of the other place. When would we be able to move in?"

"November fifteenth."

I thought I might faint! God had come through for us time and time before. What was my problem? Were we like the Israelites? When would we just trust and believe? We agreed after finding out that pets could be allowed if we kept the dog outside most of the time. Next, the work would begin.

Chapter 19:
Moving Again

With the help of some men from church, we finally moved into the house on November 15th, as planned. The stress must have taken its toll because within two weeks I was sick, just in time for Thanksgiving. I knew it was bronchitis because I had it before. This time, I seemed to be exceedingly exhausted, and I was wheezing. The doctor told me that I had asthmatic bronchitis and prescribed an inhaler. It made me dizzy to take it, but it helped the wheezing. Somehow, despite it all, I managed to crank out a decent Thanksgiving dinner for my family.

I was still doing public health nursing thirty miles away. Some friends of ours, a father and son, helped fix our car whenever it broke down. I regarded them as angels. The wife worked nearby and stopped frequently for lunch, which helped the day by giving me something to look forward to. Her visits were always a blessing to me. I worked two days a week. Phil was home with the kids, and we worked schooling around the schedule. At the time, Phil was receiving a non-service-connected VA pension. We were told to report additional income. Being a dutiful, honest woman, I reported my two days of work. Sometimes we'd have less than thirty dollars to last us two weeks. Our church pantry was helpful with the food needs.

I reported my income to the VA. Shortly thereafter a letter arrived. They decided that my income for a family of five put us over the allowable amount for non-service-connected pension and they were cutting off Phil's pension. In addition, they said we had to pay them back five thousand dollars. I was livid. I did the right thing by reporting my job and now we were going to get penalized. I called our local Congressman and submitted a letter. Thankfully, it didn't take long for a response. He had the five thousand dollars waived. I contacted the Disabled American Veterans who told me if I could find any shred of evidence that Phil had any early symptoms of MS in seven years since discharge that we might have a case to support service-connected compensation. At first, I thought this was impossible. I met him eight years after his discharge. It would be like looking for needle in a haystack.

Phil's condition was worsening. At that time, they tried putting him on Paxil for depression. He would sit in the living room and stare out the window. No matter what we did to try to involve or distract him, nothing helped. After a while they took him off the medication. He was feebler than ever.

He was using the walker. I was able to get him up the carpeted stairs into the bathroom and into the shower. That came to an end one afternoon. The kids were all gone to their friend's. I got him down the steps the usual way, sitting, and moving down with my help. The wheelchair was parked at the bottom of the steps. There, I would lock my arms around him beneath his armpits and couch, using the larger muscles in my legs. That day, the chair slid back, and Phil landed with my guidance as he slipped to the floor. No one was there to help. I propped him up safely with pillows and called some friends a few miles away. The wife answered.

"Chris? I need help. I was getting Phil into the wheelchair, and he slipped down to the floor. I'm not strong enough to get him back to the chair."

"Sure, I'll be down to help you." She replied. "I used to have to help my grandfather down south, so I know just what to do."

She came over and with one sweeping motion got him up into the chair. From that day forward there was no more going upstairs for showers. Bed baths became the ritual. An inflatable sink was placed on a towel beneath his head so I could wash his hair. The water drained through the hose into the bucket I placed on the floor.

One sweltering day, I saw him yawn. He removed his glasses and began to rub his eyes. It became too difficult for him to follow what was happening on the movie. Without asking for help, he reached his arms out in front, trying to grasp the walker, which stood too far away for safety. Turning to me, he asked a question.

"Do you think I could go rest awhile? I'm very sleepy." The polite request was replayed hundreds of times in a week.

"Of course!" I replied, moving across the room to retrieve the metal frame that had become his constant escort. Placing it in front of him, I bent and supported his right arm as he pushed with the left.

"One-two-three!"

"You did all the work again!" He exclaimed.

I reminded him that he had helped also. Now braced, and turning in the direction of the living room, he began the pilgrimage to the bedroom. Once again turning to me, as he moved and I walked behind him, he asked another question. This question had become more frequent and each time he asked it, my heart whimpered in pain. It felt like a strong wind rushing through boiling waters, burning as it moved.

"Is there a room with a bed in it for me?" I fought back the tears.

"Yes, Phil, our bedroom, where we both sleep. Do you know where it is?"

"I think it's to the left out here." His voice had become higher pitched, which was also part of the nervous disorder associated with the MS.

"That's right."

Moving across the kitchen, he looked up. His tired brow was furrowed in confusion. He shook his head to acknowledge that he was headed in the right direction. First, he went to the bathroom, the little room with the curtain hanging in the place where I had to remove the door. From there he went to the bedroom, where the white quilted pad lay neatly on its place on the bed, just in case of an accident. As he ritually did, he took his place at the side of the bed and turned the radio on. It was always on the same station as it had been for years. The melodies of singing saints invaded the stillness of the room. It was his favorite. The fan whirred its continuous saga in the window, blowing in the breeze that was just a few degrees cooler than the humid day. I felt that breeze brush my cheeks as I knelt at his feet to remove the socks. As always, in that position, I thought of Jesus being served by the woman with the alabaster box who anointed his feet with the precious ointment.

"Whatever you do to the least of these, you do unto me." I felt the presence of God, like I had so many times, and I knew His grace was helping me to ensure the moment that pained my heart. Tucking Phil beneath the sheet, I assured him that I would be in the next room if he needed me. As I turned to leave the room, the fan blew in the faintest scent of late summer air before it turns to fall.

"Another season is going." I thought. "We still wait for the season of healing to come."

Over four years had gone by. The children had become teenagers and the family station wagon was sold. I had more grey hairs on my head. I kissed his cheek and left the room.

The silence intimidated me. Fearful thoughts tried to descend and consume me. The drone of the air conditioner was my company. My body ached and I was exhausted. I put the cassette tape into the recorder. The song spoke of dancing in God's presence. A memory invaded my mind. It was only a year ago. How could it be? We had traveled to a minister's convention at the request of an elderly woman who was always encouraging us. During the worship, we had been able to dance. Where was the walker then? Had things changed that much in just one year?

The next song came on. It spoke of laying down our life. It seemed like I was always laying down my life. My legs ached, as if something was laying on my sciatic nerve. I dumped my weary body on the couch. The wet drops fell to my cheeks as I prayed for more strength to endure. I needed to continue trying to be a good mother and wife. I needed to be the "velvet-covered steel" our first pastor had long ago admonished, when we were going through the PTSD issues. There was a difference though. Then it had been both of us. Now it seemed like the weight of the world was resting on my shoulders.

One afternoon I went for a walk. The little patch of road was where I took Phil outside for his daily rides in the wheelchair. He was taking his nap that day and the children were home. I had a lot on my mind, and I needed to clear my head. I decided that I was going to try to find that needle in a haystack. If I could find any shred of symptoms within that seven-year post discharge it would help our family. I had to try. The four-year journey began.

First, I called his sisters. The youngest told me that he was blinking and twitching his eyes like crazy when he got back from Vietnam. She said he'd try to make a joke out of it.

"I bet you can't do this." He would tell her as his eyes were batting out of control. He had no choice in the matter.

I looked it up. Nystagmus was twitching of the eyes and in some cases, it was an early sign of multiple sclerosis. That was great but certainly not enough. I knew he had lived with his sister in Rochester when he came back. I also knew that after he married the first time, he had lived near his parents in the Cooperstown area. Plunging blindly, I jumped into the search. Like a detective on the prowl, I pursued. Microfilm was almost a thing of the past, but Strong Memorial in Rochester and Bassett Hospital in Cooperstown still had them. I was able to find emergency room notes in both places that Phil had been there more than once for "fever of unknown origin" and other non-specific issues. I called the DAV representative. He thought I had enough information to open the case. If we won, Phil would receive the service-connected compensation. That meant there would be regular monthly benefits for him and his dependents that couldn't be changed if I worked. The DAV representative cautioned me that it would take a long time before they approved or disapproved. In the meantime, I stayed on it with letters to the Congressman and at one-point daily phone calls to the county Veteran's affairs office. Of course, there was lots of paperwork involved, as always, with any bureaucracy.

I knew the humidity was exacerbating the MS. Our car had no air conditioner. One day I had a patient that had glaucoma. Her husband had died a year ago, and their car still sat in the garage. It was an issue of concern for her. It was a 1979 Chrysler LeBaron-a tank of a car. The mileage was low with 29,000 miles. She was selling it for fifteen-hundred dollars. It had an air conditioner and plenty of rooms for the kids. I told her my dilemma and explained how that car could help us.

"Well, the man putting a roof on that house down the street looked at it. He's thinking about it. If he changes his mind, then it's yours."

The next couple of weeks I prayed fervently that the roofer would change his mind. My prayers were answered when she called to tell me that he was no longer interested. It was the car that fell out of heaven for us!

Chapter 20:
Broken Hips and VA Trips

Phil was becoming impatient with everyone. No one seemed to be able to do anything the way he wanted it done. I continued to fight for his VA benefits as the months rolled on and his condition worsened. One day, while attempting to get out of bed with the walker, he fell onto the floor. He was moaning in pain. At first, I thought I could help him, but when we tried to move him, he cried out more. I called the ambulance. They were already familiar with us. The fire department was across the street. They eased him onto the stretcher. I followed to the emergency room. Phil was diagnosed with a broken hip. The orthopedic doctor told me surgery was required to pin the hip.

The operation went well. At first, his temperature was 99 degrees. The nurses didn't take heed. When I reminded them that he needed Tylenol, they refused.

"That's not our protocol. The Temperature has to get to 101 before we can give him anything."

Apparently, I had to educate them. I took my assertive nurse stance.

"My husband has MS. If his temperature goes up one degree, it exacerbates the MS symptoms. He needs Tylenol immediately before it makes him sicker!"

They called the doctor and got the order.

In the ensuing days, other issues arose. The hip dressing was supposed to be changed daily. When nurses change a dressing, we initial it with the date and the time. One day I checked it and it hadn't been changed in two days. Another time I found the soiled bloody dressing in the little bag attached to the rollaway table that the food was served on. Each time I complained to the staff.

One morning, I arrived later. It was past 10:00 a.m. I noticed Phil hadn't been shaven. I went to the nurse's station. They were all behind the desk looking at someone's vacation pictures. I interrupted them.

"Excuse me. It's past 10 o'clock. My husband hasn't been shaved."

The head nurse stood up, looked me straight in the eye, and retorted.

"We don't shave everyone every day."

I could feel my blood begin to boil. This was a small community hospital. The nurse-to-patient ration was 1 to 5, unlike where I was used to working where the ratio was 1 to 12. These girls had it good. This was what many of us referred to as a "country club hospital." I stared directly back and made my declaration.

"Well, my husband gets shaved every morning. It contributes to his well-being. Please shave him." They begrudgingly went in to shave the patient.

Along with everything else, Phil had an indwelling catheter, which was standard for post-operative status. Soon after the catheter was taken out, he was diagnosed with a urinary tract infection. The doctor ordered it to be put in again. I found out that they didn't even try to have him stand to void prior to this. Re-inserting a catheter would only serve to worsen the infection. In all the time I'd cared for him up to that point he never had a urinary infection. I was furious.

My anger only increased by the time he was transferred to the nursing home for rehabilitation. He still had the catheter and the urinary infection. In less than one day he developed a rash all over. They were short staffed. I was going twice a day to do his basic care. It was March and roads were still nasty from snow. I went there so many times it felt like there was a rut in the road just for me to go back and forth.

One nurse practitioner that we knew made a statement to me.

"You must be so relieved that your husband is in the nursing home."

She sparked the fire that was already burning inside of me.

"No, I'm not!" I snapped. "My husband is forty-six, not eighty-four. He is the father of three children. He belongs home! Besides, I am doing all of his care anyhow!"

She faded into the background. I never heard from her again.

Time seemed to drag while Phil was in the nursing home. He had to learn how to walk again with his walker. Since we had no parallel bars at home, the physical therapists had to work with him there. It was hard not having him home, even if he was sick. I was thankful it wasn't located in another city. The family routine was discombobulated even more. Everything had to be worked around the daily trips to the nursing home. Hardly anyone outside of the kids and I visited him. I remember asking our pastor to stop and visit him since it was on his way home from his office at the church. He did visit him. Once. I don't remember our children ever complaining. They were very supportive children despite the changes that were going on in their lives.

I decided that Phil needed a break from that place, and we needed him home. There was a local medical transport vehicle in town called SCAT van. I found out I could rent it and arranged to get my husband home for the weekend. I don't remember the price, but it was worth the effort it took to arrange it. I was the driver, and he could sit in his wheelchair secured by the tie-downs in the back. I remember teasing him when I was driving home because he had always liked to be the "in charge" driver whenever we went anywhere. Now it was my turn.

The kids had their dad home for the weekend. We made our usual Sunday trip to church and up the ramp with the wheelchair. At that time, Phil was saying "Amen" all the time and smiling politely at everyone. When I brought him back to his room at the end of the weekend, it was difficult to leave him there. I left, heart deflated, and depressed over the way the whole situation had changed our lives. Not long after that weekend, he was discharged. It was great to have him home, walking with the walker again. A physical therapist came to our home to continue the strengthening exercises.

My twentieth college reunion was coming up. It was forty-five minutes away. A woman we had known from church for years offered to come and stay with the family so I could go. She was a home health aide. Her mom was a nurse. She agreed to help her daughter. I was able to go to the first reunion ever. I had missed the high school ones previously because I had to be home to care for everyone. It was refreshing to spend time on Keuka Lake with friends from long ago. I came home feeling restored.

Soon thereafter, the day came when the MS was exacerbated. Phil needed to go into the hospital for five days to receive a run of intravenous steroids. Prednisone was the medication of choice. The meds for MS that are available today were unheard of then. I arranged for the children to be cared for. The VA hospital was still not very reliable at that time. Neither was Phil's memory. I needed to be there to be his advocate. One day the doctor met me in the hall outside of the room. His face reflected an empty look of doubt and hopelessness. Shifting his weight nervously from one foot to the other, he began to speak slowly. His words fell like deafening thunder.

"How long have you been married?"

"Eighteen years."

"Are you aware that you'll be looking at a nursing home in ten years? Your husband has multiple lesions on his brain." Clutching his clipboard, he made a weak attempt to look me in the eyes. I stood there with him, toe to toe. I looked straight at him.

"As a nurse, I'm well aware of the ramifications, but my hope is in God."

Nodding his head, he held up his hand showing me his crossed fingers, then walked away. His words bounced threateningly inside of my head, playing chase with the fear that tried to grip me. My spirit rose boldly above the emotion and claimed victory for the moment.

It wasn't until three in the morning when the hospital was quiet and Phil was asleep that the words came looming back to me, preventing my rest. Soon my sleeplessness was propelling me down the long dark corridor to the elevator and into the chapel. I had chosen hope over despair, but it was getting more difficult. I sat quietly in the peacefulness of the room, surrounded by stained glass windows. A bible was opened on a table in front of me. I needed strength that I could hold onto. I thought of our children at home with the sitter and wondered if they felt the same way. Children can't always express their feelings the way adults do. Sometimes those thoughts came out in other ways. The bad feelings had to leak out somehow. Sometimes they blamed themselves, erroneously. I seemed to sit there for a long time. A scripture finally dropped into my mind.

"Weeping may endure for a night, but joy comes in the morning."

I didn't know exactly how that would apply to our lives, but it was a smidgen of hope. I grabbed onto it like I used to snatch those dandelion wisps in the air, believing I could be granted a secret wish. The next day, Phil was discharged. The steroids had worked, and the symptoms were quieted.

Life as we knew it resumed. I was cleaning the house and vacuuming one day with my two-part vacuum cleaner. I had finished the upstairs and taken the lighter half of the machine downstairs. I lazily decided to pull the heavy canister part of it down the stairs and didn't move fast enough. It landed on my toe. The pain was worse than having a baby. My great toe swelled and turned purple. I didn't call anyone at first. My mother stopped by and convinced me that I should. When I saw someone at the fire department across the street, I called the paramedics. They came and looked and told me to get it checked out. I went to a podiatrist who took x-rays. As he showed me the results, he spoke.

"See that?" He pointed to the triangular image at the end of the toes.

"That is your toe. It is not only broken, but also crushed. There's not much we can do but let it heal."

He gave me crutches and sent me on my way. I remember our eldest son walking through the living room one day after that. Phil was in one chair, asleep with MS, and I was in the other chair with my foot elevated and the crutches nearby. Chris just looked at us, shook his head like his parents were an impossible situation, and walked on.

Eventually the toe healed. It wasn't easy hobbling around doing all the care and chores I needed to do. A wonderful older woman, Marie, from our church picked up the children and took them everywhere during that time. She even took them to see the Olympic flame when the runners passed by in a town fourteen miles away. She was such an unselfish blessing to us. Whenever anyone asked how she was, she would answer, "Thankful."

Chapter 21:
A New Chapter Begins

I tried to deny it, but Phil's condition was worsening. I tried to believe there would be a miracle. He was worn out. It was as if all his energy had left him. I was unable to motivate him for anything. The neurologist tried another idea. He put Phil on something called Cylert. It was a medication like Ritalin, for attention deficit disorder. Somehow, the doctor thought it would increase his energy. It also failed. Soon he was off that as well.

One New Year's Eve we went to church. Everyone flocked to that service because the pastor would get a prophetic word for everybody in the small church. He walked over to us. He said that he pictured our family with a cornucopia. He told us that God was going to cut the red tape. At this point I had been in constant contact with the Disabled American Veterans, who were advocating for his case. This involved writing numerous letters to whomever could help. I was going to see the Congressman regularly and calling his office daily to see if anything had progressed to help us. I had been fighting this battle for four years and though I was tired of it along with the daily requirements to maintain my family, I continued to push through. My family had to win. I wouldn't be able to work and take care of him full time. I was still home-schooling our children. I was also thankful to God for the food pantry and some people who brought us food occasionally.

A month later, in my birthday month of February, the letter came. Phil's case was finished, and he won. Though they didn't want to connect it to the Agent Orange, which was the plight of many Vietnam veterans trying to make their claim, they finally did award him one-hundred percent service connection They also made it retroactive. He was going to receive $97,000 in benefits. By this time, he was completely wheelchair bound and his talking was becoming minimal. The prophesy had come true. With that new service-connected status, his monthly VA income was going to make him eligible for a VA home health aide and help with whatever he needed for housing adaptations and medical supplies. There was nothing to do but cry. It was paradoxical. Joy lived on one side of the tears, thanks to the financial relief, and sorrow lived opposite with the physical demise due to the progression of the MS.

We began to look for a place to live. Finally, we could buy a house and no longer be subject to landlords and high rents. There would be no more asking if we could bring a pet, and we would have freedom to paint or do anything we wanted to with our home. We also would no longer be subject to eviction or being homeless again. It was a miracle.

Some people began to change when they heard about this. I found it was amazing how people can be different when it comes to money. Some were jealous. They had watched us go through so many trials. They knew we had more to go through. Others seemed to want handouts. We helped several people, as well as the church, with donations and little loans. It felt like it was our time to give back. Now we had to find a house that was accessible for someone with a disability. We needed a ranch, because Phil could no longer go upstairs. He was wheelchair bound.

One day my boys went to get their hair cut at a place they'd been going to since we moved to that city. They came back all excited. The hairdresser was selling her house. It was a ranch, only five minutes from where we already lived, in a nice area, just outside the city. It was country enough as well with an acre of land and a creek. We decided to go look at it and found that it was larger than it appeared from the front. It was a three-bedroom, landscaped property with a huge living room, small dining room, finished basement with a pool table and one and a half bathrooms. It had an inground pool and a huge pole barn in the back. There was an attic over the garage. They were asking $114,000. There was a problem with the leach field. I put an offer in for $108,000 on the condition that they would fix the issue. They accepted it. Phil was barely able to talk or make decisions. He came with me to the closing. We finally had our own home.

Now we had to move. Amongst all our stuff, we had a piano. How could we manage to do this? I decided that since we could finally afford it, I would have to hire a moving company. The children were all excited about things like the yard, the pool, and the dishwasher. I was excited to have a place where we could function with this disease and whatever it brought to our future.

The move to our new home was exciting, but bittersweet. It was August of 1997. The movers got our belongings transferred them to the new house, which was only a couple of miles away. Everyone was excited. Winning the compensation case led us to receive a wonderful home health aide. She soon became like a part of our family. She was Phil's age and very supportive and knowledgeable about her role. She always went the extra mile, helping me with the family laundry, amongst other things. She was great to talk to about anything. I felt like we not only gained more help, but a friend as well.

One of the first things that occurred was Phil's eligibility to get help from the VA to have a ramp attached to the house. The five-thousand-dollar grant paid for a wooden ramp to be built onto the front. He had physical therapy and occupational therapy in the home too. He could barely walk small distances and standing was a challenge. The therapist and I would park the wheelchair at the end of the kitchen in front of the sink. With a good boost, holding onto that belt, we would get Phil standing with our assist for a short time. Though he could hardly speak, we learned that if we started any scripture, he could finish it. His voice was very weak. That became the routine.

"Many are the afflictions of the righteous." We started each one.

"...but the Lord will deliver him from them all." Phil would complete the sentence.

It was amazing that he had such a recall for none else but his beloved Word of God that was clearly fixed in his heart. After a few of those exercises, he was allowed to sit down.

When the occupational therapist came, we would all go outside. He had a big green ball that he would use to play catch with Phil. Sometimes other family members would participate. Sometimes there were puzzles for him to do. At the nursing home, there had been writing exercises. On one such occasion, he wrote me a note.

"I love you Frances. Be happy."

Many nice days were spent sitting outside with Phil in his wheelchair, under the maple tree in the front yard. He enjoyed the shade and the outdoors. Several times I took him for walks down the road and back in that wheelchair. I would talk his ear off the whole way, pointing out things for him to see.

The day came when I began working with the Paralyzed Veterans of America. In addition to the first grant, he was eligible for a thirty-eight-thousand-dollar grant to make the house handicapped accessible by VA standards. This included adding another ramp onto the house, a new bedroom and a bathroom that was wheelchair accessible, including a roll-in shower, closet that was reachable from the wheelchair, bars in the bathroom, and wider doors on the addition. The VA regulations stated that we had to have another ramp on a different part of the house. The architects in New York City at the PVA decided that they would include an exit from the new bedroom onto a deck that went beyond the sixteen-foot width of the pool. The ramp would be at the far end that led to the inner pool area. While this was being done, since we could afford it, I arranged for the small dining room to be extended. The contractor added a tiny deck onto the dining room, predicting that I could take Phil outside in the mornings for breakfast. The construction began shortly after we moved in. The house was bustling with more changes as at the new additions went up and the construction teams went to work.

Besides therapists, nurses, aides, and construction teams, the children who were then in their early teens, had friends coming over all the time. It was never boring at our house. Chris had his Siberian husky in the backyard. Michael wanted to have a little dog. One day I went with my mom to visit a lady that was breeding Boston Terriers. The lady was selling the pups and the mother. My parents fell in love with the dogs. I bought the mother dog, Molly, for my parents, and one of the pups for us. Michael named the pup "Fuji." The tiny thing fit in our hands. Everyone fell in love. Phil enjoyed having the puppy on his lap along with a cat we had. Fuji was another addition to the busy hub of a household that was trying to find joy and humor in every day, in spite of the uncertainty of the life before us.

Days included their share of frustration. I started a support group for caregivers of those with MS. Secretly, I hoped it would help me too. It was called "Restoration." Several people came to the first meeting. The church let me hold the meetings there. I went around the group, having everyone tell their story and just where they were in their caregiving status. Surprisingly, none of them were at the place we were with the MS. Sadly, I had to acknowledge to myself that our situation was far advanced beyond the place where others were. I was also a member, at the time, of a national unit called, "The American Family Caregiver's Association." I had read in their newsletter that they had done a survey about the emotions of the caregivers. The number one on the list was frustration. I certainly could agree with that. After a couple of meetings, I didn't continue the group. I didn't feel that I was able to give much hope to the other members, considering that our situation was digressing rapidly.

That frustration level showed its ugly head frequently on mornings, which, laden with interruptions, seemed to be racing too fast. This occurred especially the days when we didn't have the aide coming. One day I knew it would be such a day. Phil had awakened early enough for me to bathe, shave, and dress him without any complications occurring. His morning smile always dismayed me. He was always ready to face his new day with silent thankfulness. It was ironic. He was quietly thankful, and I was always so frustrated.

I wheeled him down the hall to the fold-out table I had affixed to the wall for the sole purpose of having breakfast with him. He needed to be fed. Since ours wasn't an eat-in kitchen, this was the best answer. I parked his wheelchair while simultaneously getting the children's attention so they could begin their school assignments. I was interrupted by the phone. Some telemarketing campaign was in progress. It felt like it was scheduled to intrude our morning progress. Next, I retrieved the "Thick-It" from the cupboard. I began to mix it into the orange juice. He could no longer drink liquids that were not thickened, for fear of choking. A speech therapist had come to our home and determined the need for that. I prepared the oatmeal. Just as I was about to give him his first mouthful, someone knocked at the door. The town representative had chosen a great time to see if our dogs had licenses. I explained to the lady that I had forgotten to renew the licenses on time due to my business caring for my husband. She gave me some paper, telling me I had a designated number of days to comply. As hurriedly discussed this trivial nonsense, the oatmeal grew colder and Phil waited longer.

I could feel my blood pressure rising as the frustration mounted. Putting the oatmeal in the microwave and giving Phil a sip of juice, I told the kids to do their reading while they waited for me to get to them. Someone was knocking at the door again. It was our elderly neighbor.

"I want to give you a report on the town meeting I went to."

He was a very nice gentleman so I couldn't get angry at him. He went on, smiling, about the flooding problem we had with the creek that bordered our properties. I rushed him through the conversation, tapping my foot impatiently. Refraining from slamming the door at the end of his discourse, I returned to Phil, who's head was dropping to his chest as he began to doze. I had enough of the interruptions that morning. I remembered when Phil worked as a manager, he used to tell me how he learned to deal with the interruptions. I never seemed to be able to attain his level of patience. The kids finished their reading assignments. I managed to get half of the oatmeal in Phil before he lost interest in eating. I pushed him into the living room and transferred him into his lift chair. The phone was ringing again. I wanted to scream. I didn't.

Chapter 22:
Plummeting

Life became a roller coaster ride. I spent many times at the altar in church. I was either repenting for getting angry at my circumstances or begging for strength to get through whatever was to come. The children were doing well despite it all, or so it seemed to me. We had a pool and pool table. They were having their friends over. I was glad for that, rather than have them going off and never knowing where they were. Many of the friends were helpful and sympathetic towards our circumstances and I felt that it helped the children with support they needed from their peers.

By that time, I had to use a Hoyer lift to get Phil in and out of the bed and chair. The older one had been replaced with a digital one from the VA. I remember Michael taking a ride on it to see what it was like. Then I tried it out while singing.

"I believe I can fly."

Chris made an interesting comment that made us all laugh.

"When they make these things do they test them on people or lab rats?"

We found that humor, no matter how dry or stupid, was helping us get through our days. The medical equipment was taking over our house. There were constant deliveries from the VA of incontinent pads, condom catheters, and more. It progressed to medications for breathing treatments and a suction machine. Our bedroom began to look more and more like a hospital room. Our children were our constant helpers. This included getting Phil in and out of the car. Chris was often the one to lift him before the VA helped us get a conversion van that we could put the wheelchair in. The kids loved that because they could watch movies in it. I loved it because occasionally I would go outside and sit in it for a break from reality.

There were times that things accelerated at such a fast pace that I didn't think I could ever keep up with them. Fear was always trying to grip me and snatch away my faith. The slow downhill roll left me doubtful and depressed, ready to give in to the lies the enemy fed into my fears. Nights became long and sleepless. Through it all, God was faithful. The days were peppered with little bits of encouragement and promises.

One tumultuous time began with Phil having a little cold. He had more congestion and therefore more difficulty breathing and swallowing. His chest sounded like an endless rattle at night. Attempts to clear it seemed futile. I found myself trying to cough for him. I felt helpless, except for the little strength I had to try and roll him over on his side and cup my hands over his lungs. It was ironic. That was what he did to the patients in the intensive care unit when I met him. Each time he managed a cough my heart sang a victory song. Then off to sleep we would drift, but not for long before the rattling sound of trapped saliva woke us again. I tried chest rubs and set him up on Pillow Mountain to help him breath more freely. I had learned these things as a nurse. Minutes dragged into the early morning hours and every cell in my body cried for rest.

I called the doctor. He complied with my first call and made a home visit, stating that Phil had postnasal drip. He prescribed cough syrup. My stethoscope hung on the bedpost, on call at my demand. My next call to the doc was for an antibiotic because the rattling had continued for two more days. He complied again. Two more days and I was demanding a chest x-ray. I found myself having to fight to get the results. The doctor's secretary told me it was a "possibility of infection."

"That is no x-ray report."

After vain attempts to get results, I called the director of nursing at the VA. She said she was unable to find out what the problem was. I made up my mind I was going to get reports that day. I called the radiologist myself, ready to grab his throat through the telephone line. I informed him that I was the patient's wife, power of attorney, and a registered nurse. I also told him I was fully aware of the freedom of information act in New York State. He quickly said he'd get the file and came back with the report.

"Linear densities in the right lower lobe, possibly indicative of early pneumonia or atelectasis." He read to me on the phone.

Atelectasis! That was a collapsed lung. I knew something had to be done fast. My every waking minute was spent trying to keep my husband from getting any complications that would further deteriorate his condition. I was back on the phone with the primary doctor, who prescribed a stronger antibiotic. The next day I was calling for orders to get respiratory therapy, calling the Pastor for prayer, and calling God to give me wisdom, keep me awake, and heal Phil quickly. I ended up with albuterol nebulizer treatments to administer to him. I also ended up with anger towards God and fear of a tracheotomy as I fought my way through the days. I was thankful for the word, "Stand." In my weakest moments that kept me going.

"Stand. Having done all to stand."

I was doing everything I could think of, but I had to trust God during my lack of understanding. There were days when I even doubted the promise of standing. I wondered about this anguish, this Hell. When would deliverance come for him, and for all of us? The days went on, so slow and difficult. We prayed, hoped, and prayed some more. I felt for my children, longing to lift this nightmarish life, hoping somehow it would make them strong. Some days I cried and cried until the tears dried up and the heart broke. I needed to see. We all needed to see something.

May came. One day, movement outside the window caught my eye. At first it registered in my mind as snow, but it was May 3rd. Sixty-five was way too warm for snow. The motion danced before my eyes again. Gracefully falling from somewhere above, a plethora of bright pink crab tree blossoms cascaded in front of my window. The vision of falling flower petals enthralled me. It was such a simple thing. I was amazed amidst my doubts and frailties, hardship and failures. God managed to allow my senses to capture that moment. After almost dropping Phil on the floor, crying my heart out to God, and thinking that He'd gone on vacation, He still managed to demonstrate His mercy and beauty to me. It was more than amazing. It was silent, yet profoundly loud. Without doubt, times like that were the highs that got me through to the next challenge.

Chapter 23:
Against Hope, He Believed in Hope

This whole experience put into perspective the things we take for granted. I remember watching Phil lift his hand as he usually did to brush back his hair. His hands trembled on their way to his head, advancing on their mission. Then they stumbled along the way to his lap. It was such an effort. He tried again. Instinctively, I reached out to guide them to that place where they were destined. When I let go, the tremors took over, causing his hand to pound mercilessly against his head. Then, still shaking, they retreated to the place where they rested on his lap. I thought of how those hands had helped and comforted me, and how they had wiped my tears in the past. Once, those hands had typed poems to me and held our children, tossed the ball, and cooked meals for us. I realized how much I missed them. I realized how I had taken them for granted.

More memories flooded in through the months. I thought of them as something found in the attic of our life. In the attic I searched and found dust had begun to collect. I found walks in the sunshine and snow. There was laughter and singing, a rented piano and candlelit dinners. There was the winged-back chair where our life began together with talks that lasted for hours. I saw dancing and the look that used to melt me. There were nights when we worked at the hospital and shared our breaks at four in the morning. Boxes of poems he wrote me were stacked neatly between hikes at Mendon Ponds and trips to Brooklyn. I remembered the time he told me the Star Market grocery store became the Taj Mahal when we were together. I realized that the attic held the keys to us that must never be forgotten. I knew I'd go back several more times in life.

Soon it was August of 1998. I had to pry his arms open so I could sit on his lap. I looked at him from the resting place of my head on his shoulder. He stared into space. The music played. It was a song about getting away together. It was about all the things we never got to do. The tears forced their way out of my heart. I tried to catch them before they reached his shoulder. I told him I missed him and needed him. His eyes closed, then opened again. That was his way of saying he heard me, since his words came very seldom anymore. All I could do was hold him and wish he could tell me he loved me one more time.

Labor Day brought a furious storm with it. They said it wasn't a tornado. It was a microburst, something I'd never heard of. Tanya and Michael were at the State Fair with friends. Chris was in his bed. It was 11:00 pm. Phil was bathed and tucked into bed, Hoyer lift at the side. I sat on the edge of the bed, exhausted, and about to get some sleep. The thunder was rolling in quickly, along with intense, frequent lightning flashes. I had just sat down when suddenly the wind was on top of us. I didn't have enough time to get Phil out of bed, into the wheelchair, into the stair glide, and down the stairs. I laid on top of him and prayed while the wind howled, and the thunder roared.

When the noise stopped, I ran into the hall to find our son. I was automatically praying out loud.

"He who dwells in the secret place of the Most High shall abide under the shadow of the Almighty."

Thankfully, Chris had recently moved his bed to the other side of the room. It was under the window before. A tree had crashed into his room through the window. There was glass everywhere, but he was unhurt. There were branches through the basement window. Branches and leaves were in the house. Two of the vendors at the Fair got killed in the storm. Tanya and Michael couldn't get home. A house, struck by lightning, caught fire and the road to get home was blocked. They stayed at a friend's house that night. I was so thankful they weren't hurt or stuck somewhere on the road. We wouldn't see the extent of the damage until morning.

When the sun rose, our street looked like a war zone. Our whole backyard was filled with giant fallen trees, many of which were on our roof. Huge branches had crashed into the pool, breaking the chain link fence that was around it. The streets were not passable. The power was out. Later, the news told us there had been wind gusts up to 115 miles per hour. 200,000 people in Central New York were in the dark. Neighbors drew together, calling each other on cell phones and going to work to clean up. Those with generators were fortunate. The rest of us used what ice we could get to keep our food from spoiling until the electricity came back on. Phil's lift chair wouldn't work but we were able to get him into it. The challenge of cleaning the yard, calling the insurance company, and getting the trees off the roof piled onto the everyday duties. My sons and others went to work with chain saws to clean up the debris.

September came quickly. I found myself praying for grace more frequently. Every day I'd get Phil into that Hoyer lift and back to bed for a nap. He was sleeping more. His eyes looked so heavy from fatigue. He would look up at me and smile with those big blue eyes and moments later, they closed, and he was snoring. Occasionally he would say something. His words were precious. I wrote them down on the calendar. Once we had a mini conversation.

"Too much." He said while he coughed again to prevent choking on his saliva.

"Too much what?"

"All of this is too much."

I cried again, wanting so much to help but not knowing what else I could do. I tried to encourage him by telling him what a wonderful husband and father he was. I talked to him about some of our early memories and told him what a unique person he was. He was generous, sensitive, giving, caring and wise. I felt that he needed to hear those words.

His left foot was swelling. The imprint of my finger stayed when I checked. In nursing lingo it's called "pitting edema." I knew it wasn't a good sign. He struggled just to take a sip of the juice I would try to give him in the sippy cup. Since he could no longer lift his arms, I had to feed him and give him drinks all the time. I missed him so much. I wondered if others knew that just to be able to talk to your spouse was a blessing that shouldn't be taken for granted.

On November 9, 1998, he spoke a whole sentence.

"Frances, I'm going to need you." The words fell into my ears like lead bricks. I sensed that it was a forewarning of some kind. A quiet pleading.

Halfway through November the geese were flying South, and it was getting colder outside. I had just finished talking to the children about "comfort measures." Phil had been very quiet for the prior couple of days. One day I was getting him ready for his nap I asked him a question.

"Are you afraid?"

He shook his head that time. It was a resounding answer.

"Yes."

Then I asked him to try and tell me what he was afraid of. He couldn't say another word. The seasons were changing, and I was afraid. My mind wandered.

"Will he be here for Thanksgiving next week?"

"Will he be here next year at this time when the seasons change?" I told him that day that I will love him forever and that there will always be a big part of my heart with his name on it. No one would ever be able to fill that space except him.

While I was in the kitchen one day preparing lunch, I was listening to a tape. I had found the cassette stuck in a seat in a van our pastor had gotten us before we got the conversion van. It was a sermon. The preacher was talking about Shadrach, Meshach, and Abednego. They were headed for the fiery furnace. They said something to the king that struck my heart loudly.

"Surely, the Lord is able to deliver us, but if not..."

It couldn't have been any louder. It was as if God himself was in my kitchen talking to me. Something inside my chest rose into alert and then was overtaken by a great peace. I knew I had to trust God. Surely God was able to heal Phil, but if not, I had to trust God that He knew what the outcome would be. I continued to hope against hope, like Abraham. I had that scripture posted on my refrigerator. I wanted to believe that no matter how dark it looked, God could still turn the whole thing around. Hearing that sermon about the three Hebrew children was a vector that carried me through the months to come.

Chapter 24:
Holidays Come and Go

We made it through Thanksgiving. It was rough because Phil was sleeping most of the time. I recalled our first Christmas in the new house. I hosted. The basement had a stove and refrigerator. We put up an artificial tree down there and decorated the place with lights. The pool table was covered with a huge piece of plywood and tablecloths. We had furniture down there. The guests could mill around between upstairs and downstairs. We were excited to be able to host in our new home. Phil was able to go downstairs with the help of the stair glide. I had bought it from someone in town. The men that did the construction put it in for me as soon as the addition was completed. I was able to cook upstairs and keep the food warm in the downstairs oven. We lined up tables in the dining room. My sister and her husband from Colorado were coming, along with other family members and friends. Regardless of the MS, it was a memorable event.

Fast forward to Christmas of 1998. Phil was very sleepy. He fell asleep in his wheelchair at the table. I brought him into our room and put him into bed. He was sleeping more and more. It was nice to have the family together for emotional support. That Christmas was very taxing and full of tears. On Christmas morning, Tanya did her yearly reading from the book of Luke about the morning Jesus was born. We all tried to be normal but there was a melancholy cloud hanging over the holiday.

New Year's rang in with more news. At 1:30 a.m. on December 27, Thomas, my stepson, and his wife arrived from Florida. Phil's eldest son, David, was already here from California. They hadn't seen their dad in a long time. There is no lack of sense of humor in this family. True to form, when Tom got in the door and saw his brother, it was one joke after another. It got serious when Tom announced that his wife was going to have a baby. Everyone swooned and went to bed awhile later.

The next day we exchanged gifts again. The kids gave me a family ring with all six birthstones. Phil was in his lift chair with his glasses on. He received a crocheted lap blanket from his sister. One of the boys got our Boston Terrier, Fuji, going in crazy circles while she chased the laser light that he was moving in all directions. The visit went well. Soon everyone flew off to their home in the other states.

January 1999 was upon us. New Year. New hope? It was getting more difficult to hope in the face of the reality before us. Uncertainty and bone-weary exhaustion were taking over. It was getting harder to see Phil suffer through more. I kept praying for him to be comforted and for the rest of us to have strength. I struggled, trying to be strong for everyone, yet I was bumbling. Nights were long. There was now a suction machine in our room, and I had to use it regularly on Phil. Often I had to get up in the night and change the soaking diaper and bed pads. I refused to leave him wet and get skin problems. I argued with God some more.

"What glory is there in this? We are all so very tired." I tried to stand, tried to believe for a miracle but didn't see any improvements happening. I was constantly asking God to forgive me for my shortcomings.

"I don't know what to ask anymore. I've asked so many times and tried to be honest about everything with you!

Please bring relief! Please help Philip!" The words stormed out of my mouth.

We moved further into the month. He slept and slept. We had held our breath through November because of birthdays and holidays. He had seen Dave and Tom. His daughter, Rabeccah had been up to visit in our previous house. I was happy that he saw 1999 when it rolled around. Phil's fatigue was relentless. He hardly ate or drank much of anything for two days. He would hold food in his mouth, then spit it out. Once I tried to clear his mouth so he wouldn't choke, and he bit my finger. There was no more saying "Amen" like he used to, and he hardly shook his head in response to questions. Even his eye-blinking was less frequent to respond. He stared blankly at me and often didn't answer in any way when I tried to ask things. I kept telling him I loved him and how thankful I was for him.

I was perplexed. I was distressed. I could feel depression trying to pull me down and choke me. Then I would think about how he must be feeling, and I would fight. The house had a strange silence. Some of us had been sick. It was as if strength was waning from everyone, depleting as time went, like a slow dripping faucet. I found pictures of the previous year's holidays and burst into tears when I saw the difference. The change in one year was astounding. He was less and less. His hands could hardly move anymore. I prayed for mercy and strength while my heart was breaking.

February 9 came. He spoke.

"You understand."

"I understand what?" I questioned.

"You understand the times." He responded.

"You must have been reading my mind." I told him, since I was thinking at that moment of the status of it all and wondering what was coming.

"Yes." He stated in a very weak voice.

Then he said an interesting sentence. It was simple, but profound and amazing that he could even say it.

"I was thinking about how people get jealous about material things and what matters is little things, like 'I'm happy when you eat supper."

"I like to hear what you have to say." I told him.

"Okay." He said, nodding his head slightly.

On February 24, I sent an email to my three stepchildren.

"Dad is not doing well. He is down to 144 pounds. On January 6, he was 160 pounds. A year ago, it was 186. He is having more trouble swallowing and sleeping more than ever. I asked the doctor for an all-night intravenous since he is taking less than ten ounces of fluid every day. Sometimes he only has one or two very small meals. The doctor tells me we can't give him the IV because the fluids will not go where they are supposed to, and it will be very uncomfortable for dad. I discussed a feeding tube. The doctor told me this too would be very uncomfortable for him, causing him to feel bloated and not really nourishing him at this point. Please pray for him not to suffer anymore. Last night I suctioned him for three hours straight. He is in bed more. He is serene and occasionally smiles, except when he is experiencing the secretion problems. Then he cries out and moans. I am crying every day.

Today the kids have a meeting with our pastor and the social worker to try to get them to voice their feelings. God is with him. A couple of weeks ago I asked him if he was going to go home to Jesus. He lowered his eyes, like he does when he says, 'Yes.' All who meet him say they can see God is with him. His Christian witness still goes forth. He loves you all very much. Call anytime. It is only a matter of time before your father gets a miraculous healing on this earth or goes to meet the Lord. There he will be healed forever."

Life was solemn. March came. It was March 4. I was doing a lot of thinking. As I watched the snow continue to fall and blow, I thought about life.

"That's what life is like, I thought. We blow from here to there, and then we're gone. Just like the snow that accumulates today and is melted away tomorrow. Only the memory remains."

The kids called me to my room. The pine tree had fallen.

"My, how the mighty are fallen." I thought.

That old, tall, broken pine had been leaning since the Labor Day storm. Now, with the creek flooded beneath it, there must have been little to hold the roots up. It had finally succumbed to its resting place on the ground. My eyes were swollen, and my heart was heavy. I had just gotten off the phone with the neurologist, who had informed me that he thought the time was getting close. He told me once kidney failure set in, it would only be a matter of days. I knelt at the bedside, touched Phil, read him scriptures, and asked God to help us not be afraid. All of this was after I held him, clinging to him and telling him that I want him to be happy and there would never be one who could take his place in my heart. I told him that the kids and I would be ok. I told him that I would instill in our children what was important to him.

Then I asked God for something special. I told him that the blessing I would like is that if he decided to take Phil home, that he would infuse in us all the Godly characteristics of Phil. That would include his love, boldness, wisdom, and desire to serve. I believed with all my heart that God would answer this prayer. I still prayed for Phil to be healed on this earth, but I asked for help to trust and allow whatever was God's will to be done.

I looked outside again. Even though the pine tree was down on the fresh blanket of snow, the branches on top were still waving in the wind. They were still praising God, even at that moment. I knew that Phil would be praising God forever. I only wished that I could hear him singing.

Chapter 25:
After the Pine Tree Fell

Snow covers the ground, but it can't cover the memories. They push their way into my thoughts like the first crocuses of spring. I kept trying to bat them down, knowing that I had to face them. It used to be more difficult. I didn't want to face it, but I knew that the only road to healing was through the pain.

March continued. Phil was digressing, eating only teaspoons of baby food. Strength to swallow was difficult and declining. Trying to get fluid into him was a chore. When he said good-bye to baby food, it was good-bye to all food in this world for him. His breathing grew more difficult. Suctioning was more frequent. His days from bed to dining room were few. His weight was plummeting. Our son lifted all five feet-eleven inches from the bed like a cradled baby and placed him in the second lift chair someone had loaned us.

Finally, the chair sat alone. Phil was too sick to get out of bed anymore. The electric bed from the VA was his place to rest. I remember adjusting the head and foot to try to make him more comfortable. I realized that it was all I had left to do. The weekend came. I was only able to get him to take eight ounces of fluids over 3 days. I felt frantic and helpless. He was slipping away before my eyes. If only he could talk to me. I moistened his lips with lemon flavored swabs and turned him tenderly to wash him. On Friday night, the Hospice nurse watched him so I could get a little break. I returned to hear that he had been having more changes in his breathing. He would breathe a few times, then stop for long periods of time. As a nurse, I was familiar with Cheyne-Stokes breathing. My fear was increasing, and I seemed helpless to do anything to stop it. I kept calling on the Lord for strength.

Saturday, he took a plunge for the worse. I remember calling people. Our house began filling. By Saturday night, my parents, Pastor, and his wife were here. Furniture was re-arranged. Some was brought into our bedroom so visitors would come and sit and pray for a miracle. Early in the evening, I was in the kitchen on the phone. Pastor called me into the bedroom. Angst grabbed my heart. It felt like something was trying to smother me. The pastor's voice was urgent. It looked like Phil was leaving us then. His breathing became more erratic. The children and I kept telling him that we loved him. I don't know why, but he stayed that night. I put on worship songs and tried to sing. He always liked it when I sang. It strengthened me when I could barely hold on. Without being able to talk to each other, I was just guessing what he might have wanted or needed. His beautiful eyes were glazed over, never to be clear again. I touched him frequently, as if my touch had some hidden power to make him better. That night the Hospice nurse gave him the Roxanal, which was liquid morphine, reserved for this time. In end-of-life terms, this was to keep him comfortable. Was he in pain? Was he aware of what was going on?

"I can't be the nurse anymore. I just want to be the wife." I squeaked the words out between tears that kept dripping like relentless rain. Seven years of caregiving were ending. I stared long at my thinning fifty-year-old husband. I saw a once-strong man, clad in a white tee shirt and diaper, lying on the bed.

Sunday his eyes opened again, and his older children called to talk to him. As I held the phone in his ear, and they spoke, his clouded eyes moved, as if he understood. More people came over to visit. One long lost vet friend showed up with another from the Vietnam Veterans organization. Pastor and his wife took vigil in chairs at the foot of the bed. My parents remained and stayed that weekend at our house. They were an enduring support. I put more music on for Phil and sang along with it.

"You are my hiding place. I will trust in you." I sang along as loud as I could. The children came and went, taking turns talking to him. Our daughter was nineteen and the boys were seventeen and fourteen years old.

I told the nurse again that he looked uncomfortable. He gave him the medicine. It seemed like even with the morphine, something was just not right. The swishing white sound of the oxygen machine played regularly. There was no more urinary output in the catheter bag, just orange crystals. I fought an invisible enemy. Everything I had tried so hard to prevent was happening.

"Stop!" I screamed, but it was inside. I felt like I was in a silent movie, screaming as I was falling from a cliff. No one heard me.

I prayed for God to help him. The night wore on. His heart ticked too fast at one hundred-twelve, then one hundred-twenty. His blood pressure remained steady. I cried out to God, but I couldn't sense His presence. Finally, I knelt by the side of the bed, angry, I placed my hands on Phil. I told God and everyone else that I was going to pray all night if that's what it took to help him. I still thought I could somehow fix things.

At two o'clock, I awoke, still kneeling at the bedside. It was evident that there was no relief for Phil. Agonal, laborious breathing continued. I wanted to plug my ears, run out of the room, and yell hysterically. My children fell asleep somewhere between the bed and the wall. Even with oxygen and morphine, breathing came fast and so hard. There was nothing more to calm him, nothing to touch this horrendous heavy effort at breathing. It looked more difficult than labor.

"Help him!" My mouth dry, going through this desert experience.

Finally, into the wee hours of Monday morning, breathing calmed down. I called the neurologist at 8 o'clock in the morning

"Just keep up with the medication, as needed," he said.

I went and looked at Phil's eyes. His pupils were fixed. My objectivity was lost. The doctor had to tell me.

"He's in a coma now."

No long-awaited, hoped for miracle seemed to be coming. I continued to plead.

"Please God, for the children's sake, prove yourself faithful. They've prayed so much for a healing."

Phil's heart was still racing. I wished that the rest of his body could be as strong as his heart.

Monday, more friends came and went. The children broke down crying. The hospice nurse was going to stay all night. Our daughter and I were up on the bed next to Phil. The boys were on the floor, next to the door to the deck. Mom and dad were in and out. I was glad they stayed over. Mom kept giving me words of strength. It was a quiet night. It was too quiet.

At two o'clock, the nurse checked the blood pressure. It was low. Phil's heart kept pumping. We all fell asleep for a while. Gracious Philip was still taking care of us, making sure we had some rest before he left. Then the rude intrusion of the nurse's voice jolted us from sleep.

"His pressure is falling. It's at fifty..."

Damn it! I wish I wasn't a nurse. Then that news would have had less meaning to me. I took his radial pulse and got nothing. His breathing was slowing. I put my ear on his chest and heard nothing.

"Kids, he's going now." I warned.

They started to cry.

"I love you. I love you daddy. We'll be okay. We love you."

The nurse spoke again.

"He's gone."

Crying and holding him we found we had no Phil to comfort then. He was gone. Forever. He left this world that hurt him, and he was gone. That moment took him away. He was with God, gone to the place where he was never afraid to go. He was where we couldn't see or hold him again. He was gone to a place where Vietnam couldn't touch him, and where I couldn't do anything to get him back. Silence. Oxygen was turned off. I closed his eyes forever.

I knew I must make phone calls to Pastor, funeral director, stepchildren. I dutifully did this while my husband lay, gone, in the bedroom. We moved quietly around the house. It was 4:55 Tuesday morning on March 16, 1999. At 4:55, our friend, Rick, twenty miles away, was awakened with a directive to pray for our family. And some say there is no God. With God there are no coincidences.

The day nurse came. She asked me gently.

"Do you want to help me get him washed?"

"Of course." I replied.

For the last time, I took the wet cloth and washed my husband's body. Hundreds of times I had done this while he was alive. Now he couldn't feel it. My feelings dictated my thoughts as I tried to cope.

"Now I am washing a shell."

We put a clean tee shirt on him. My heart felt gray and empty. The children and I said good-bye again. We left the room. The undertaker arrived. I knew they were taking him away forever. I knew I would sleep alone for the first time in twenty years. I would never have to puree food and stay awake all night suctioning anymore. It was the end of this journey.

The hearse left the driveway. I went into the bedroom. Emptiness I had never known moved into my heart. An unfillable void moved into me. All I could do was look around the room, hear the silence, and cry.

Now I look for him in my children and grandchildren. Reflecting now, there is a scene that warms my heart and makes me smile. In the scene, my family is in the car, enroute to the in-laws. Somewhere, between Hartwick and Oneonta, evergreen trees grow thick upon the hills. We come to the base of the hill. It's always the same place. He pulls the car over, looks at me, and smiles.

"Are you ready?" He cranks up the radio, gets out of the car, and opens my door. He takes my hand and leads me outside of the vehicle. He slips his arm around my waist. This isn't the first time. The children are delighted once again. We move to the music, while the evergreens look on. I know now why, sometimes in my dreams, we are in a faraway place, and we are dancing.

The other day I visited his place at the cemetery. A pinecone had fallen to the ground. I picked it up, rolled it around in my hand, inspected it, then gingerly placed it on the ledge of the pink granite stone. The pine trees stood at order towering above me. I whispered the word again as I turned to go.

"Evergreen."